Cambridge Elements

Elements in Phonology
edited by
Robert Kennedy
University of California, Santa Barbara
Patrycja Strycharczuk
University of Manchester

PSYCHOLINGUISTICS AND PHONOLOGY

The Forgotten Foundations of Generative Phonology

Naiyan Du
Baiko Gakuin University

Karthik Durvasula
Michigan State University

CAMBRIDGE
UNIVERSITY PRESS

Shaftesbury Road, Cambridge CB2 8EA, United Kingdom

One Liberty Plaza, 20th Floor, New York, NY 10006, USA

477 Williamstown Road, Port Melbourne, VIC 3207, Australia

314–321, 3rd Floor, Plot 3, Splendor Forum, Jasola District Centre,
New Delhi – 110025, India

103 Penang Road, #05–06/07, Visioncrest Commercial, Singapore 238467

Cambridge University Press is part of Cambridge University Press & Assessment,
a department of the University of Cambridge.

We share the University's mission to contribute to society through the pursuit of
education, learning and research at the highest international levels of excellence.

www.cambridge.org
Information on this title: www.cambridge.org/9781009532907
DOI: 10.1017/9781009347631

© Naiyan Du and Karthik Durvasula 2024

This publication is in copyright. Subject to statutory exception and to the provisions
of relevant collective licensing agreements, no reproduction of any part may take place
without the written permission of Cambridge University Press & Assessment.

When citing this work, please include a reference to the DOI 10.1017/9781009347631

First published 2024

A catalogue record for this publication is available from the British Library

ISBN 978-1-009-53290-7 Hardback
ISBN 978-1-009-34762-4 Paperback
ISSN 2633-9064 (online)
ISSN 2633-9056 (print)

Additional resources for this publication at www.cambridge.org/EPHO_Durvasula

Cambridge University Press & Assessment has no responsibility for the persistence
or accuracy of URLs for external or third-party internet websites referred to in this
publication and does not guarantee that any content on such websites is, or will
remain, accurate or appropriate.

Psycholinguistics and Phonology

The Forgotten Foundations of Generative Phonology

Elements in Phonology

DOI: 10.1017/9781009347631
First published online: December 2024

Naiyan Du
Baiko Gakuin University
Karthik Durvasula
Michigan State University

Author for correspondence: Karthik Durvasula, durvasul@msu.edu

Abstract: Research over the last few decades has consistently questioned the sufficiency of abstract/discrete phonological representations based on putative misalignments between predictions from such representations and observed experimental results. Here, we first suggest that many of the arguments ride on misunderstandings of the original claims from generative phonology, and that the typical evidence furnished is consistent with those claims. We then narrow in on the phenomenon of *incomplete neutralisation* and show again that it is consistent with the classic generative phonology view. We further point out that extant accounts of the phenomenon do not achieve important desiderata and typically do not provide an explanation for either the phenomenon itself, or why there are actually at least two different kinds of incomplete neutralisation that don't stem from task confounds. Finally, we present new experimental data and our explanation that the phenomenon is an outcome of planning using abstract/discrete phonological knowledge.

Keywords: abstract/discrete representations, planning effects, incomplete neutralisation, tone sandhi, Huai'an Mandarin

© Naiyan Du and Karthik Durvasula 2024
ISBNs: 9781009532907 (HB), 9781009347624 (PB), 9781009347631 (OC)
ISSNs: 2633-9064 (online) 2633-9056 (print)

Contents

1 A Discussion of Foundations   1

2 Incomplete Neutralisation   20

3 Our Explanation for Incomplete Neutralisation   38

4 The Current Experiment   49

5 Conclusion   69

    References   75

1 A Discussion of Foundations

There has been a fair bit of experimental work, particularly since the 1990s, trying to argue against abstract and discrete views of phonological representations. The results presented in favour of such arguments usually involve putative misalignments between predictions from phonological theories and the observed phonetic measurement. Although such observations stem from multiple experimental realms (production, perception, neurolinguistics, etc.), in this Element, in order to keep the text to a manageable length, we will focus on arguments coming from production wherever possible.[1]

We first briefly discuss the relevant orignal discourse in research espousing abstract and discrete representations within the generative phonology tradition in order to present a corrective to what has become a common understanding, and point out that much (if not all) of the research arguing against abstract representations rides on a misunderstanding of some of the original claims within the generative phonology tradition, what we term *classic generative phonology*. Subsequent to the previous broader discussion, we detail how the debate has played out with respect to the phenomenon of *incomplete neutralisation* and show again the error in the arguments against classic views of abstract and discrete representations. Furthermore, the proposed counter-hypotheses often *account* for the data purely because they have many more (sometimes thousands more) degrees of freedom; however, we will argue that they don't *explain* the phenomenon of incomplete neutralisation. In order to make progress on the issue, we list a set of desiderata and explananda that any explanation of incomplete neutralisation should meet. Next, we point out that, in addition to incomplete neutralisation stemming from non-phonological sources, there are actually at least two different kinds of incomplete neutralisation that don't stem from task effects/confounds: (a) one that is more typical and with a small effect size, (b) a second one that is a previously unrecognised variety with a large effect size that appears to be possible in the case of optional processes. Finally, we present new experimental data and our own theoretical claims that explain the two different types of incomplete neutralisation as outcomes of two different but related planning effects. As we will elaborate later, the kind mentioned in (a) stems from what we call *incremental unitary planning effect* and the type in (b) stems from what we call *simultaneous multiple planning effect*. The proposed explanations are consonant both with discrete/abstract phonological representations and the desiderata we lay out.

---

[1] Having said that, we believe the arguments and the discussions carry over naturally to perceptual and neurolinguistic evidence, as we suggest in the Conclusion of this Element.

As we mentioned earlier, before discussing the issue of incomplete neutralisation, we present a general lay of the land with respect to phonological representations. Broadly speaking, there are at least three types of theories of phonological representations that have been discussed in the last seven decades or so: (a) exemplar theories that propose detail (high-dimensional) lexical representations that have no discretisation within a lexical item either in space or in time (Bybee 2001; Goldinger 1996, 1998, amongst others), (b) theories that propose representations within a lexical item that are abstract and discrete both in time and in space (Chomsky and Halle 1968; Halle 1959b; Postal 1968, amongst others), and (c) hybrid models that incorporate both abstract/discrete and detailed representations (Pierrehumbert 2002, 2016, amongst others).[2] We intend the following discussion to be both a relevant background for the rest of the Element and a corrective to the view of abstract/discrete representations that is commonly argued against in modern experimental work. For this reason, we include many relevant quotations of some of the original claims.

1.1 A Brief Look Back at History

To start off, it is important to note that, while exemplar theories are typically discussed as reactions to theories of abstract/discrete representations, this is far from true. In fact, Silverman (2012) presents a detailed exposition of Kruszewski's (1883/1995) view, which sounds almost exactly like modern exemplar theories. Of course, one should always be careful of anachronistic attributions when talking about research that is 140 years old, but as Silverman points out, Kruszewaki is quite explicit in some instances about his stance, as observable in the in the following quote.

> The spontaneous changes of a sound depend on the gradual change of its articulation. We can pronounce a sound only when our memory retains an imprint of its articulation for us. If all our articulations of a given sound were reflected in this imprint in equal measure, and if the imprint represented an average of all these articulations, we, with this guidance, would always perform the articulation in question approximately the same way. But the most recent (in time) articulations, together with their fortuitous deviations, are retained by the memory far more forcefully that the earlier ones. Thus, negligible deviations acquire the capacity to grow progressively greater... (Kruszewski 1883/1995, pp. 51–52, as cited in Silverman 2012).

---

[2] There are of course many interpretations of each of these three broad theories, and of course many other representational theories such as articulatory phonology (Browman and Goldstein 1988, 1989, 1990, and subsequent work). However, they can be seen as a selective mixture of properties seen in the three basic theories listed. We elaborate on more specific theories/hypotheses in the context of incomplete neutralisation later in the Element.

Notably, Silverman (2012) suggests that Kruszewski's (1883/1995) views were/are all but forgotten, and that 'many subsequent scholars ... have clearly been unaware that certain of their insights are prefigured – or, sometimes, fully explicated – in Kruszewski's work' (Silverman 2012, p. 330). However, from a certain perspective, one can rationally argue that exemplar models are what might be called obvious models,[3] since these models are closest in form to the actual perceptual input or production output. So, it would be somewhat surprising if researchers espousing abstract/discrete representations in the mid 1950s and after were not aware of the possibility, particularly given the climate of behaviourism (Skinner 1957, amongst others) and the severe purely inductive empiricism of that period that those espousing abstract/discrete representations were reacting to (see Chomsky 1959). Indeed, a close look at the research by generative linguists of that period and after shows that they were aware of such a possible view. In fact, Morris Halle's work in the 1950s–80s, despite not citing Kruszewski as far as we are aware, repeatedly argued against detailed high-dimensional acoustic/articulatory information as forming the basis of lexical and phonological representations. Two representative quotations are given in the following from long before exemplar representations became popular in modern phonetic work (also see Halle 1954, 1959a, b, 1962).

> I begin with the negative assertion that it is unlikely that the information about the phonic shape of words is stored in the memory of speakers in acoustic form resembling, for instance, an oscillogram or a sound spectrogram. (Halle 1985, p. 122)

> Thus, Professor Singh regards the model of language in which features and phonemes play a central role as just one among several more or less equally plausible alternatives, while we have tried to argue – in our review and elsewhere – that the evidence for this model is so over-whelming that all other models must be regarded as unlikely possibilities. We are well aware of the difficulties that the phonemes and features model has encountered in attempting to account for certain perceptual and articulatory facts. These difficulties, however, are rather small when compared to those that every model lacking phonemes and features encounters in trying to account for the most elementary linguistic fact, e.g.; the plural rule of English. (Halle 1978, p. 279)

While the second quote doesn't directly talk about high-dimensional or gradient representations, we added it specifically because Halle indirectly

---

[3] Note, we do not mean to say such models are the 'simplest', just that they might be considered obvious.

recognises that there is a small benefit to high-dimensional representations in that they can account for 'certain perceptual and articulatory facts' – that is, there is a subtle but rational debate of different representational theories that he alludes to. However, he indirectly suggests that those problematic 'certain perceptual and articulatory facts' have non-phonological explanations. Furthermore, the second quote also makes it clear that the rejection was not simply based on opinion or philosophical intuitions or 'intuitive appeal', as some have suggested (Nixon and Tomaschek 2023), but based on empirical arguments about what can be considered fundamental aspects about sound patterns in human language. We expand on these fundamental aspects about sound patterns in human language in the following subsection.

Given the rather extensive discussion and arguments in support of abstract and discrete representations both in Halle's work and others' work in the 1950s and 60s (Chomsky 1965; Postal 1968), we are not entirely sure of why this myth of the novelty of exemplar representations as a reaction to abstract representations has continued. It is simply not the case that Halle (or, for that matter, Chomsky or Postal) is forgotten or unrecognised, unlike perhaps Kruszewski. Furthermore, we believe presenting exemplar representations as newer theories or reactions to abstract/discrete representations has led to a subtle rhetorical effect of implying that the abstract/discrete representational claims are 'old' and therefore naturally moribund. In reality, as we have already pointed out, the generative phonology framework was actually itself a reaction to the logical possibility of high-dimensional and gradient lexical/phonological representations, based on empirical considerations about the fundamental nature of sound patterns.

1.2 Arguments in Favour of Abstract/Discrete Phonological Representations

1.2.1 The Argument from Simple Morpho-phonological Patterns

As previously mentioned, Halle repeatedly presented arguments that suggest the need for abstraction and discretisation both in time (what we will also refer to as *segmentation*[4]) and in space (what we will also refer to as *featurisation*) to account for even simple and everyday morpho-phonological generalisations. Take, for example, the regular English pluralisation pattern in (1). There is no

---

[4] Note, by using the term *segmentation*, we don't necessary imply that the discretisation is in terms of segments but just that there be temporal segmentation or chunking. The segmentation can be in terms of segments, or x-slots or moras or syllables, . . . or potentially multiple different temporal windows simultaneously.

doubt that speakers (even preliterate children of the right age) know this pattern and are able to employ it on novel items as has been known since some of the earliest experimental work in linguistics in the modern era (Berko 1958).

1. The regular pattern of plural formation in English
   (a) [ɪz] before [s z ʃ ʒ tʃ dʒ] (e.g., busses, causes, bushes, garages, beaches, badges)
   (b) [s] before [p f t k θ] (e.g., caps, cuffs, cats, fourths, backs)
   (c) [z] elsewhere

As Halle (1959b, and subsequent work) pointed out, such an everyday pattern actually shows the need for discretisation both in space and time. The fact that only the last segment of the stem is relevant for the pattern shows that the phonetic signal is discretised into segment-sized chunks, (i.e., discretisation in time), and the fact that different aspects of the final segment are relevant for the disjunctive choices shows the necessity of introducing abstract features that can be shared by different segments (i.e., discretisation in space). Furthermore, while Halle doesn't discuss it explicitly, the fact that words are decomposed into morphemes, and that the morpheme-edge is the locus of the pattern shows that there are other discretisations of the phonetic signal. Of course, though modern phonologists have discussed many other phonological patterns, including reduplication, metathetis, epenthesis, deletion, and others (see Kenstowicz 1994; Kenstowicz and Kisseberth 1977, for examples), the basic thrust of Halle's argument remains the same in all of the phenomena, namely, there has to be discretisation/abstraction of the phonetic signal in space and time to account for the knowledge that speakers have. We are aware of no reanalyses of such patterns without appealing to discretisation in space and discretisation in time. Furthermore, many such patterns are clearly productive for speakers of languages, and therefore cannot be relegated to artefacts of history that remain in the lexicon.

1.2.2 The Argument from the Existence of Alphabetic Writing Systems

A second argument Halle repeatedly provided is the observation that alphabetic writing systems with (roughly) segment-sized characters are replete across the world. This constitutes evidence that temporal discretisation is natural for speakers of languages; a fact that would not make sense if lexical and phonological representations were detailed phonetic traces. In fact, as far as we know, there are no writing systems that reflect the detailed phonetic information that is claimed by pure exemplar representations – we (the authors) find it difficult to even imagine such a writing system that might be useful to a user. One might of course counter this observation by arguing that alphabetic writing systems evolved just once and for typographic convenience, and some have argued that the use of alphabetic notation for phonological representations ultimately stems from the fact that European linguists were influenced by European orthographies (Firth 1948; Öhman 2000; Port 2007). For example, Port (2007) states that "[T]hese compelling intuitions about how to describe sound [in terms of segments[5]] are... *a consequence of our* [i.e., linguists[6]] *lifelong practice using alphabets and not a necessary psychological fact about speech*" (p. 351, italics in the original text).

However, similar alphabetic intuitions for phonological descriptions have been observed even in non-literate societies. For example, even pre-Pāṇinian Sanskrit grammarians/phoneticians (circa, at least, 700 BCE) used segmental and featural abstractions despite not having an orthographic system at all, let alone an alphabetic system (Allen 1953; Lowe 2020). Furthermore, Lowe (2020) points out that even the orthographies that the pre-Pāṇinian Sanskrit grammarians/phoneticians might have been in contact with did not mark vowels (and many other aspects which the grammarians marked quite consistently). So, the descriptive tradition of the Sanskrit grammarians/phoneticians was not only independent of an influence from orthography, it was in fact inconsistent with any orthographic system they might have been aware of.[7]

1.2.3 The Argument from Neogrammarian Sound Change

A third argument in support of abstract/discrete representations comes from modern phonological work on historical phonology stemming from observations of wholesale Neogrammarian sound change (Kiparsky 1968). The fundamental point to be observed about Neogrammarian sound change is that it affects all words with the relevant abstract segments. Note, if there is no segmental (or featural) abstraction, it is difficult to see what yokes different words such that they change en masse over a period of a few decades/centuries. This problem is also highlighted by Goldrick and Cole (2023) in their review of different theories of lexical/phonological representations as a challenge for exemplar representations. Furthermore, it was already realised even before

---

[5] Added by the current authors.
[6] Added by the current authors.
[7] It is not anachronistic to impute claims of psychological reality to their phonological representations, since there is a rich history of discussion of psychological reality in that tradition (see Allen 1953; Coward and Raja 2015; Lowe 2024).

the modern re-advent of exemplar representations that, even to account for wholesale Neogrammarian change across contexts, one needs some sort of abstract/discrete *context-independent* representations.

> In support of the claim that this abstract phonetic level has psychological reality and cannot be dispensed with, one might bring to bear the following sort of argument. In spite of the obvious acoustic differences between the two [b]s of Bob, we are justified in identifying them because we have good evidence that the language user does. In historical sound change, such classes of distinct acoustic signals as initial and final [b] are often grouped together as focus or conditioning environment of the change. When speakers invent symbols for the perceived sounds of their language, the members of classes of this type are not distinguished. (Kahn 1976, p. 29)

1.2.4 The Argument from the Recombinant Nature of Phonological Representations

The quotation from Kahn (1976) also alludes to a fourth fundamental property of lexical and phonological representations, namely, that of the recombinant nature of such representations. Evidence from synchronic and diachronic sound patterns suggests that the same (segmental) representations appear in different positions of a lexical item, and are sometimes affected in synchronic and diachronic sound patterns in a context-independent fashion.

1.3 Two Competing Views of Phonetic Manifestations and Associated Auxiliary Assumptions

The fundamental properties of sound patterns discussed form the evidentiary basis for the need for abstraction or discretisation of time (segmentation) and space (featurisation) as discussed by generative phonologists over the years. Again, we are unaware of any explicit reanalyses or counter-explanations of both synchronic and diachronic phenomena by those who argue against such abstract representations.

In contrast to these observations, others have argued for high-dimensional and gradient representations based on observations such as the following: (a) the phonetic distribution of a target changes in response to new variants (Dell et al. 2000); (b) recent experiences to specific words affect later pronunciation differentially on whether the word is a high-frequency or low-frequency word (Goldinger 1998); (c) word-specific phonetics (Wright 2004); (d) lexically conditioned sociolinguistic variation, wherein the view that exemplars encode lexical, phonetic, and social information simultaneously provides a mean for expressing the interaction of each of these dimensions (Hay et al. 1999). We present these observations here to help the reader get a better grasp of the ensuing discussion, but request the reader's patience in waiting till Section 1.4 for a more elaborate discussion/criticism of their putative import for theories of representations.

Returning to the issue at hand, while the adduced fundamental properties of sound patterns are evidence in favour of abstract/discrete lexical and phonological representations, they say nothing about how the representations manifest in performance (in the phonetics, in this case). As has been long noted, theory testing depends not only on the actual theory, but also the auxiliary hypotheses that are additionally needed to interface the theory with observed phenomena (Duhem 1954; Lakatos 1970; Quine 1951). Consequently, it is useful to distinguish between two different (and incompatible) conceptions of how abstract/discrete representations manifest in performance: one that has become the *de facto* standard and the whipping boy for those arguing against such representations, which we will call the *common strawman view of discrete representations*,[8] and one that was intended in the original generative phonology tradition, which we will call the *classic generative phonology* view.

As per the *common strawman view of discrete representations* view, the interface between phonology and phonetics is a feed-forward system where the (categorical) form of the output of the phonology, that is, a surface representation, *wholly determines the phonetic outcome*. In this view, phonology is seen as an abstraction of the actual production of an utterance and can therefore be seen as production-oriented. This view has been explicitly mentioned and argued against in work supportive of exemplar representations (Goldrick and Cole 2023; Pierrehumbert 2002, 2016).

> In modular feed-forward models, the (categorical) form of the lexeme wholly determines the phonetic outcome. If two words differ at all in their phonetics, then they differ categorically, and accordingly one job of the phonology is to identify a category set which captures all systematic differences amongst words. (Pierrehumbert 2001, p. 101)

> In such theories, the phonetic realization of a word is determined entirely by its phonological representation. (Pierrehumbert 2016, p. 45)

In fact, we agree with Pierrehumbert and other proponents of exemplar representations that the *common strawman view of discrete representations* is very likely wrong. However, an argument or evidence against a specific instantiation

---

[8] In previous work, we have called this the *standard generative phonology* view; however, we don't actually know if this view is held by most phonologists, and have ourselves largely seen it only in research arguing against abstract/discrete phonological representations; hence, we found it appropriate to relabel the term.

of how abstract/discrete phonological representations interface with the phonetics is not in fact an argument or evidence against the *whole class* of possible instantiations of how abstract phonological representations interface with the phonetics, and claiming so would be an error of logic – as we can't rule out that the evidence actually bears on the auxiliary assumptions, and not on the main theoretical claims themselves.

Furthermore, and crucially, the view discussed, which we called the *common strawman view of discrete representations*, though often presented as **the** generative phonology view is ironically in contradiction with the framework of *classic generative phonology*, but unlike the latter, has never been explicitly argued for as far as we are aware. Therefore, it is a strawman that no one that we know has truly argued for; hence, our term for it.

As per *classic generative phonology*, phonology is seen as *knowledge* (or *competence*) that can be used during performance. This is the classic distinction between *competence* and *performance* that has been discussed repeatedly in the linguistics literature (Chomsky 1964, 1965; Schütze 1996; Valian 1982).

> Linguistic theory is concerned primarily with an ideal speaker-listener, in a completely homogeneous speech-community, who knows its language perfectly and is unaffected by such grammatically irrelevant conditions as memory limitations, distractions, shifts of attention and interest, and errors (random or characteristic) in applying his knowledge of the language in actual performance. To study actual linguistic performance, we must consider the interaction of a variety of factors, of which the underlying competence of the speaker-hearer is only one. In this respect, study of language is no different from empirical investigation of other complex phenomena. (Chomsky 1965, pp. 3 – 4)

Note, like the strawman view, the classic generative view also espouses a feed-forward model, but of a slightly different kind. The distinction that Chomsky draws not only relies on the idea of knowledge of language (competence) and the use of that knowledge (performance), but it also makes it absolutely clear that competence (abstract/discrete lexical and phonological knowledge in our case) is only *one of the factors* affecting performance. However, despite the rather clear discussion in the early work, there has been some confusion about the distinction between *competence* and *performance*. Competence has often been interpreted to mean an abstraction over the *performance*. While there is a sense in which this is appropriate, stating it this way also leads to a misunderstanding that competence is simply abstracted production. In our opinion, the appropriate way to parse the distinction is to say that competence is knowledge that is *separate* from other factors that are involved in actual performance.

> ...it is perhaps worth while to reiterate that a generative grammar is not a model for a speaker or a hearer. It attempts to characterize in the most neutral possible terms the knowledge of the language that provides the basis for actual use of language by a speaker-hearer. When we speak of a grammar as generating a sentence with a certain structural description, we mean simply that the grammar assigns this structural description to the sentence. When we say that a sentence has a certain derivation with respect to a particular generative grammar, we say nothing about how the speaker or hearer might proceed, in some practical or efficient way, to construct such a derivation. These questions belong to the theory of language used the theory of performance. (Chomsky 1965, p. 9)

A final aspect of the classic generative view that is relevant for our purposes has to do with 'psychological reality'. While in our opinion, the term *competence* has been interpreted to mean abstract, and not being psychologically real, it was meant to stand for abstract as being separate and real from other factors.

> ...mentally represented grammar and UG are real objects, part of the physical world, where we understand mental states and representations to be physically encoded in some manner. Statements about particular grammars or about UG are true or false statements about steady states attained or the initial state (assumed fixed for the species), each of which is a definite real-world object, situated in space-time and entering into causal relations. (Chomsky 1983, 156–157)

These quotes make it clear that the classic generative view, and more specifically the *classic generative phonology* view are quite removed from the claims of what we have called the *common strawman view of discrete representations*. One might object that Chomsky's views were never meant for phonology. Although, we don't see how that is possible, it is clear that similar discussions can be found in relation to phonology specifically. For example, as Hammarberg (1982) puts it specifically in the context of discussing phonology:

> It [generative grammar] is a competence model, not a performance model, and what the relationship between the categories and the activities of the vocal tract or auditory system might be is virtually unknown. It is highly doubtful, however, that performance could be viewed as another component of the grammar, added after the phonology, spitting out segments in the manner of a line printer in relation to a computer. (Hammarberg 1982, p. 134)

In fact, early generative phonologists could not have been any clearer on this point. For example, the following is a quote from Postal (1968) that Chomsky and Halle (1968) approvingly cite:

> ...the derivative knowledge a speaker has about the pronunciation by virtue of his knowledge of the superficial syntactic structure of the sentence, the lexical items or formatives it contains and the rules of phonology... The phonetic transcription... is the most gross and superficial aspect of linguistic structure... It [phonology] is the most important but far from the only parameter determining the actual acoustic shape of the tokens of the sentence. (Postal 1968, p. 274)

Furthermore, Chomsky and Halle (1968) state explicitly after discussing Postal's quotations outlined that they do not view the phonology (and thereby phonological representations) as capturing all aspects of the phonetics of the actual utterance.[9] As can be seen from the following quote, they even argue against what we have called the *common strawman view of discrete representations* view.

> Our conception thus differs from an alternative view that the phonetic transcription is primarily a device for recording facts observed in actual utterances. That the latter view is not tenable, in any very strict sense, has been known at least since mechanical and electrical recordings of utterances have revealed that even the most skillful transcriber is unable to note certain aspects of the signal, while commonly recording in his transcriptions items for which there seems to be no direct warrant in the physical record. (Chomsky and Halle 1968, p. 293)

Here is one final quote[10] from Mohanan (1986) that very explicitly states that phonological knowledge is just one of the factors that affects the performance (phonetics).

> Practitioners of phonology often distinguish between internal evidence, which consists of data from distribution and alternation, and external evidence, which consists of data from language production, language comprehension, language acquisition, psycholinguistic experimentations of various kinds, sound patterning in versification, language games, etc.... The terms 'internal' and 'external' evidence indicate a bias under which most phonological research is being pursued, namely, the belief that the behaviour of speakers in making acceptability judgments is somehow a more direct reflection of their linguistic knowledge than their behaviour in producing language, understanding language, etc. This bias appears to be related to the fact that linguistic knowledge is only one of the inputs to language production, language comprehension, and other forms of language performance. What accounts for the facts of performance is a conjunct of a theory of linguistic knowledge ('What is the nature of the representation of linguistic

---

[9] Note, in our opinion, a total account of the acoustic (or any performance) is something that one can't even hope to achieve in principle anyway.

[10] Thanks to Scott Nelson for giving us the quote.

knowledge?') and a theory of language performance ('How is this knowledge put to use?'). (Mohanan 1986, p. 183)

As the reader can see from these quotes, the real claim as per the *classic generative phonology* is: *all things being equal*, two representations with the same phonological content must have the same performance (phonetics). But, it is immediately clear that two identical lexical representations or two surface representations with differences elsewhere are not expected to have exactly the same performance characteristics (or phonetic manifestations). Therefore, showing evidence of non-phonological effects (for example, frequency effects or effects of sociolinguistic knowledge or speaker-sensitivity . . . either in production or in perception) in no way undermines the *classic generative phonology* view. Of course, the need to identify what elements of performance come from the abstract knowledge a speaker possesses and what come from other factors makes the enterprise more complicated; however, this complication was always seen to be necessary as per the *classic generative phonology* view (see Chomsky 1965, 1955/1975; Chomsky and Halle 1965, for extended discussion).[11] Furthermore, while researchers may/do disagree about what comes about from the phonology or lexical representations (i.e., *competence*) and what comes about from other performance factors, there is in our opinion agreement that multiple sources of influences exist on any performance; that is, there is tacit agreement for a distinction between *competence* (in this case, phonological knowledge) and other performance factors for all researchers. Consequently, everyone (and not just those espousing abstract/discrete representations) needs to worry about the different possible sources of any performance output. So, we don't see this as a problem for abstract/discrete representations alone, but a general scientific problem for anyone interested in phonological representations/computations. Therefore, we are at a loss to explain why the dichotomy between *competence* and *performance* has evoked such strong reactions in the literature.

One could complain that the presence of an *all things being equal* clause makes the theory unfalsifiable. However, that is not true, as the theory predicts some important (fundamental) aspects of speech patterns. Furthermore, as Lakatos (1970, p. 175), one of the pre-eminent philosophers of science in the twentieth century, clearly states, 'one can easily argue that ceteris paribus

---

[11] Note, saying two representations with the same phonological content must have exactly the same performance (phonetic manifestations in our case) is like saying two sentences with the same syntactic structure should have exactly the same performance (processing) and should not be affected by aspects of the lexical items or the meanings of the words, . . . – such a view is too simplistic in our opinion, and was never part of the classic generative thinking.

[*all things being equal*[12]] clauses are not exceptions, but the rule in science'.[13] He further argues that only a 'dogmatic falsificationist' would interpret inconsistency between a specific scientific theory and facts as falsification of the theory. Unfortunately, this is exactly what has happened in the case of arguments against abstract/discrete representations, despite the original proponents being rather clear that their conception of the *classic generative phonology* view had an implicit *all things being equal* clause attached to it.

So, whence does the difference in the two views of generative phonology come? We suspect that the *common strawman view of discrete representations* arose from a misunderstanding of the classic claim that phonology is a *feedforward system*, which means that there is no feedback from performance systems back to phonology. However, this term has been misunderstood to mean that *only* the output of phonology affects phonetics, that is, performance is sensitive only to the output of phonology. In this latter view, generative phonology is viewed as a sort of production system, which is contrary to the original claims of generative phonologists. Relatedly, researchers already worried (in the 1970s) about the term *generative grammar* being misunderstood along the above lines.

> There seems to be considerable confusion on this issue, due mainly, we believe, to a misinterpretation of the term 'generative' (as in 'generative grammar', 'generative phonology') as meaning 'creating', 'bringing about'. It is this misinterpretation that gives rise to views of competence as merely idealized performance, or of performance as an additional component of a grammar. (Hammarberg 1982, p. 135)
>
> It is important to interpret the term generate in a static, rather than a dynamic, sense. The statement that the grammar generates a particular sentence means that the sentence is one of the totality of sentences that the grammar defines to be grammatical or well formed. All the sentences are generated, as it were, simultaneously. The notion of generation must be interpreted as would be a mathematical formula containing variables. For example, in evaluating the formula y^2+y for different values of y, one does not say that the formula itself generates these variant resultant values (2, when y = 1; 5, when y = 2; etc.) one after another or at different times; one says that the formula generates them all simultaneously, or better still perhaps, timelessly. The situation is similar for a generative grammar. Although one sentence rather than another can be derived on some particular occasion by

---

[12] Added by the current authors.

[13] Note, this is in effect no different from a physicist arguing that the effect of a gravitational force (or space-time curvature in more modern conceptions) is that of attraction – this prediction is only true *all things being equal*. If, however, there is a repulsive magnetic force also present, then the prediction is clearly not true. We use this example from physics simply because we believe our target audience is likely to be familiar with such a straightforward case.

> making one choice or another at particular places in the grammar, the grammar must be thought of as generating all-sentences statically or timelessly. (Lyons 1974, p. 1002)

Our (some might say, painstakingly long) discussion with the inclusion of specific quotes is not to show deference to authority. Instead, we show that the arguments laid out by those who espouse exemplar or hybrid views, in our opinion, do not actually argue against the entire class of possible abstract/discrete phonological representations, or for that matter the actually espoused view in generative phonology work on the topic. What they actually argue against is a rather specific production-oriented view of the interface between phonology and phonetic manifestations that was already thought to be 'untenable'.

1.4 Arguments Proposed in Favour of High-Dimensional and Gradient (Exemplar) Phonological Representations

At this point, one needs to ask what is the sort of evidence that researchers have presented in support of high-dimensional and gradient lexical/phonological representations. In what follows, we briefly review the evidence furnished, but we direct the reader to a wonderful recent review article on the topic by Goldrick and Cole (2023). They categorise the evidence into four distinct groups, which we follow here:

2. Evidence for exemplar representations within the realm of speech production

    (a) The plasticity of production, wherein the phonetic distribution of a target changes in response to new variants (Dell et al. 2000).
    (b) Lexically conditioned phonetic plasticity, wherein recent experiences to specific words affect later pronunciation differentially on whether the word is a high-frequency or low-frequency word (Goldinger 1998).
    (c) Lexically conditioned phonetic variation, wherein there can be word-specific phonetics (Wright 2004) – as an additional example, they suggest the phenomenon of incomplete neutralisation, which we focus on later in this Element.
    (d) Lexically conditioned sociolinguistic variation, wherein the view that exemplars encode lexical, phonetic, and social information simultaneously provides a means for expressing the interaction of each of these dimensions (Hay et al. 1999).

In reference to (2a–2b), as far as we can see, both of these observations are about how and under what conditions learning proceeds, and not about the representations themselves. Therefore, they don't constitute evidence in favour of any kind of representations, per se. One should be able to take the same learning strategy and employ it with different kinds of representations. So, if learning of lexical representations is possible beyond a certain age, one can account for (2a), and if one can store more than one abstract/discrete representation for a lexical item, and the more recent ones are more accessible, one can account for (2b). Essentially, the reason exemplar representations can account for such phenomena is tangential to the issue of the discrete/abstract nature (or lack there) of the representations, and instead has to do more with auxiliary assumptions related to learning that are added to the theory. Note, this is perfectly consistent with the *classic generative phonology* framework, wherein phonological knowledge is just one source that affects performance.[14]

In reference to (2c–2d), we do think these arguments get at representations but are not actually pitting abstract representations versus exemplar representations. Again, the arguments in our opinion really ride on auxiliary assumptions tacked on by researchers. Abstract representations are usually assumed to have the auxiliary hypothesis of singular or unitary lexical representations, while exemplar representations by their very nature consist of multiple tokens. But, as mentioned, one can easily imagine abstract representations where lexical items can be linked to more than one representations, and equally one can imagine high-dimensional representations which are unitary (perhaps as a prototype). So, yes, if a speaker is constrained to store only a single abstract representation for a morpheme, then one might have to think more carefully about how to account for the fact. However, if a speaker can store multiple possible competing underlying representations for the same morpheme, then the issue of lexically conditioned (sociolinguistic) phonetic variation is not problematic, as one can easily envision lexical items with different sets of abstract

---

[14] Relatedly, a reviewer asks what exactly is a lexical representation if more than one abstract/discrete representation for a lexical item is possible. Bromberger and Halle (2000) include some discussion about what a lexical representation is. They point out that though phonological representations are normally understood to be intentions, this cannot be the case for underlying (or lexical) representations since the intention is not executed in many cases (due the application of phonological processes). Ultimately, they argue that underlying representations play a computational role. They 'essentially simplify computations within the theory'. (Bromberger and Halle 2000, p. 28). Note, such an understanding of lexical representations being purely mental devices to simplify computations doesn't preclude the possibility of multiple abstract/discrete representations for a lexical item. In fact, to our knowledge, the claim that a lexical item *has to have* only a single phonological representation has not been theoretically or empirically justified; it has simply been assumed by some. We raise this issue to shine a light on the need for more justification of this assumption.

representations for different superficially similar morphemes, and consequently would expect different phonetic manifestations.[15]

Given the previous discussion, we suggest that in fact much of the evidence presented in favour of high-dimensional and gradient (exemplar) representations is largely tangential to the issue of the nature of phonological representations. Furthermore, given that such representations do not have an explanation for the obvious and fundamental properties of sound patterns we discussed (as seen, for example, in plural formation in English), we ourselves see the weight of the evidence against such representations.

Relatedly, Pierrehumbert (2002, 2016) observes that pure high-dimensional and gradient (exemplar) representations do not have an account of speaker behaviour with nonce words: 'To support the processing of novel word forms as well as familiar word forms in novel contexts, an abstract level of representation is needed in which many phonetic details and contextual features are disregarded'. (Pierrehumbert 2016, p. 33).[16]

Furthermore, she points out that lexically-specific effects are quite small in comparison to the generalisation effects seen in such experiments, which would be surprising if lexical representations were truly exemplar in nature. Despite the acknowledgement of the advantages of abstract/discrete representations over high-dimensional and gradient (exemplar) representations, Pierrehumbert (2002, 2016) ultimately proposed a hybrid model, which has both categorical representations for each word, and word-specific phonetics. This was so because she also accepted that the evidence furnished against abstract/discrete representations (see the evidence for exemplar representations in (2)) was convincing. However, the evidence furnished is only incompatible with the *common strawman view of discrete representations* view (as her quotes make clear). As we noted, the observed data is perfectly compatible with the *classic generative phonology* framework. Therefore, we don't see the evidentiary necessity for hybrid models, ourselves. More generally, again as pointed out earlier, arguing against a specific theoretical instantiation of a general framework can't argue against the whole class of theories consistent with that framework, since there are a variety of auxiliary assumptions that could be blamed (Duhem 1954; Lakatos 1970; Quine 1951). In our case, it is clear

---

[15] This is true particularly if the phonetic manifestation is seen as a result of an averaging effect over mutliple competing underlying representations and consequently multiple competing surface representations. We elaborate on this more in the context of incomplete neutralisation.

[16] We point out here that this is not only a problem for the production of, but also the perception of nonce words. If speech perception is seen simply as an act of identifying the best lexical item match in high-dimensional space, there should never be the percept of a nonce word in the first place. The very fact that speakers can recognise a nonce word input suggests that lexical access is mediated by the recovery of a more abstract phonological representation.

that the auxiliary assumption that phonology *wholly determines the phonetic outcome* that is a part of the *common strawman view of discrete representations* view is the locus of the problem, and not abstract representations themselves.

1.5 Consistency Is a Weak Result, but It Gets Weaker as the Space of Possibilities Increases

At this point, one can rightly contend that just saying there is no inconsistency between a theory and a certain set of observations is rather weak. However, if we unpack the claim that lack of inconsistency between a theory and observations is a rather weak result, we will see that it affects all three types of representational theories (abstract/discrete phonological representations, high-dimensional and gradient (exemplar) representations, and hybrid representations).

Let's say there is just discretisation of time (segmentation), and let's say there are just forty-five phonemes; then, even if we limit words to be seven segments or under, we would have a huge space of lexical representations, namely, $\sum_{n=1}^{7} 45^n \approx 382$ billion possible words.[17]

Now, if we allow for both discretisation of time and space (so, segmentation and featurisation), then with just twenty binary features, we would have $2^{20} = 1,048,576$ possible segments,[18] and consequently, $\sum_{n=1}^{7} 1048576^n \approx 1.4 * 10^{42}$ possible words of seven segments or fewer – an astronomically large set of possibilities. So, the reader can see that consistency with a theory is rather weak.

But the problem is simply worse if we have thousands of continuously varying phonetic parameters (see Port 2007, for discussion of the size of the parameter space with exemplar representations), and even if the phonetic parameters are constant within a roughly segmental duration, we'd leave the domain of a finite size and move even past countable infinity to an uncountably infinite set of possible words.

So, with just discretisation in time or with discretisation in time and space, the problem of indeterminacy and its logical cousin, falsifiability, are rather acute (Chomsky 1965; Hale et al. 2007), but the problem of falsifiability is even more compounded when we enter the world of rich multi-dimensional structure in the domain of real numbers as is necessary when we talk about

---

[17] We limit ourselves to discussing the space of lexical representations and ignore the space of phonological patterning to keep things fair in comparing the three types of representational theories – pure exemplar-representation based theories have no explicit claims about how phonological patterning is achieved, which itself is quite problematic of course.

[18] This assumes underspecification is not possible. If it is possible, then the number grows to $3^{20} = 1,048,576$ segments. See Reiss and Volenec (2022) for an identical combinatoric calculation over features.

high-dimensional and gradient (exemplar) representations, and even further compounded when we talk about hybrid representations. Consequently, as a logical matter, the claim of compatibility between theories with high-dimensional and gradient representations and observed data should be *even less* convincing than that between abstract representations and the same facts. Yet, we see researchers have argued the contrary. In fact, Port (2007, p. 360) recognises a version of this combinatorial problem with segmental categorical representations; in his argument, with forty-six phonemes and words of five or shorter, there are '228 million' possible words,[19] and the problem 'gets far worse very quickly' with longer words. Yet, his solution that 'the relevant space is... probably thousands of degrees of freedom' (p. 350) seems to us to exacerbate the problem far more, as we discussed earlier. Therefore, while we agree with the criticism that there is a need for further explanation of the observed phenomenon beyond claims of consistency with the theory, we think the problem worsens if one espouses high-dimensional and gradient (exemplar) representations.

To add to the discussion, in the last few decades phonologists have argued for (a) a more structured feature space, namely, feature geometry (Clements 1985; Sagey 1986, amongst others), and/or (b) a more limited featured space based only on contrast that are used in lexical representations (Archangeli 1988; Dresher 2009; Halle 1959b; Steriade 1987; Trubetzkoy 1969). If we impose either of these theoretical constraints on an unstructured abstract/discrete feature space, we are likely to reduce the dimensionality, and therefore reduce the space of possible segments and the space of possible lexical representations. In both cases, the exact reduction in hypothesis space will depend on the nature of the proposal of course. For example, if say seven features are enough to represent the contrastive segments of a language (and are enough to account for the patterns observed in the language), then with seven binary features, we would have 128 possible segments – a much smaller set of segmental possibilities; and consequently, $\sum_{n=1}^{7} 128^n \approx 34.6 * 10^9$ possible words of seven segments or fewer – a smaller set of possible lexical items. The point we would like to draw attention to is that with a sufficiently rich UG (or innate constraints), the astronomically large set of segmental possibilities and lexical items can be tamed with discretisation in space and time. To achieve a similar reduction in the space of possible words, a theory with high-dimensional/gradient representations would need to impose an even stricter set of innate constraints, that is,

---

[19] We are unsure of whether there was a mathematical error or if it was a typo, but the answer should have been $\sum_{n=1}^{5} 46^n \approx 210$ million.

increase in the representational space comes at a premium. In short, there is 'no free lunch' (Wolpert and Macready 1997).

Although we have so far proceeded with the assumption that high-dimensional and gradient (exemplar) representations can account for or are consistent with the observed facts, it strikes us that discussions of such representations are often vague on the details of the precise nature of these high-dimensional and gradient representations: What exactly are the dimensions and how exactly do they interact? Compare this to the rather specific set of features/representations proposed in generative phonology (see Chomsky and Halle 1968; Kenstowicz 1994, for examples). In the absence of specific hypotheses about the relevant dimensions and possible interactions, it is difficult to see if high-dimensional and gradient (exemplar) representations are even consistent with the observed data. In our opinion, it is in fact the vagueness of the relevant claims that allows one to claim consistency. Note, a researcher espousing abstract/discrete representations could also have argued that if you inflate the number of featural representations (from the usual twenty or so features) to perhaps an unspecified list of fifty features, they can account for the observed data.[20] It is immediately obvious that such a move is unfair. But the same criticism should then apply to cases where researchers argue for high-dimensional and gradient representations but don't provide the exact representations or possible interactions. Ultimately, both the modifications appear consistent with the observed data, but the views only *appear* to be successful since they are vague.

Finally and related to the above discussion on high-dimensional and gradient (exemplar) representations, a sufficiently elaborate model/account can always account for any data by essentially overfitting the data. However, it is not the case that such a model *explains* the data. What we can all agree to is that a theory should *explain* the facts (to the extent that we think the facts need an explanation); but for that, we need to be clear about what one means by an explanation and how it contrasts with just a non-explanatory model or a non-explanatory account of the facts; a distinction that has been central for ages in the philosophy of science (see Cummins 2000, as it applies to the cognitive sciences). The latter are just redescriptions of the data, while the former are claims about the underlying causal structure. Crucial to the distinction is that if a theory is truly an explanation of a phenomenon, then the theory will *entail* the phenomenon (all things being equal), or in probabilistic terms the theory will make the phenomenon much more likely than the absence of the

---

[20] In fact, as Reiss and Volenec (2022) point out, even twenty features is actually enough if one is creative with their use.

phenomenon (all things being equal). That is, a theory is explanatory to the extent that it predicts reality (but not the converse of it, or its absence even). We believe this necessary aspect of aspiring for *explanatory* theories is missing from many of the current discussions, which are at best talking about consistency of a theory with some phenomenon, and are not saying anything that is even falsifiable in the worst case. Take for example, the observation of structure-dependence in syntax that has become an important explanadum in recent discussions (Piantadosi 2023) – deep neural networks ('large language models') trained on vast amounts of human language data show similar patterns of structure-dependence, and this observation has been used to argue that modern language models are themselves *theories* of language, and more specifically syntax. However, such claims are misplaced since they are simply redescriptions of the data that they were trained on. Crucially, if one were to give a modern language model data that is not like human language at all, in that the sentential patterns do not exhibit structure dependence, then such a 'large language model' would very likely learn the patterns present in that data and not learn structure-dependence – that is such models do not truly *explain* why human beings exhibit structure-dependence in language, even in the face of relatively little relevant input, in the first place (see Chomsky and Moro 2022; Chomsky et al. 2023; Moro 2016, for related discussion).

Given that we are ultimately calling upon researchers to make very specific testable hypotheses that generalise to other independent cases, in the rest of the Element, we plan to focus on a domain of empirical research which has featured prominently in the discussion of the nature of phonological representations, namely, incomplete neutralisation. In the spirit of the previous discussion, we will first discuss various claims in the literature and then show that despite previous claims to the contrary, the facts are not only consistent with abstract/discrete representations, particularly the *classic generative phonology* view, but we will also propose a specific set of testable hypotheses that in our opinion *explain* the phenomenon.

2 Incomplete Neutralisation

With the previous section as backdrop, we turn to a specific example where the debate over (abstract or high-dimensional/gradient) phonological representations and phonetic manifestations has raged for a few decades now, namely, the issue of incomplete neutralisation. As an example, in German, the phonological voicing contrast for obstruents has been traditionally argued to be neutralised in some contexts (we follow Michael Wagner (2002) in the claim that the process happens at the right edge of a prosodic word). A rule-based mapping of the relevant phonological process is stated in (3). However, some have argued through production and perception experiments that the neutralisation is incomplete phonetically (Port and O'Dell 1985; Roettger et al. 2014, amongst others). More specifically, derived voiceless stops have a realisation that is in-between that of underlying voiced stops and underlying voiceless stops, but with a distribution that almost overlaps with underlying voiceless stops. As will become crucial later, 'over-neutralisation', wherein derived voiceless stops have a distribution beyond that of underlying voiceless stops (such that it is the underlying voiceless stop realisations that are in-between that of underlying voiced stops and derived voiceless stops) is never observed.

3. German Final-Devoicing Rule
   $[\text{-sonorant}] \rightarrow [\text{-voice}] \ / \ \underline{\qquad}]_{\text{prosodic word}}$

We turn to this issue of incomplete neutralisation for two basic reasons: (a) there are some concrete proposals to account for the phenomenon that we can assess, (b) since at least the mid 1980s, the effect of incomplete neutralisation has been very well discussed for a variety of processes and in a variety of languages including American English (Braver 2014), Catalan (Dinnsen and Charles-Luce 1984), Dutch (Ernestus and Baayen 2006; Warner et al. 2004), Eastern Andalusian Spanish (Gerfen 2002), Japanese (Braver and Kawahara 2016), Korean (Lee et al. 2023), Lebanese Arabic (Gouskova and Hall 2009), Moroccan Arabic (Zellou 2013), Polish (Slowiaczek and Dinnsen 1985; Slowiaczek and Szymanska 1989), Russian (Dmitrieva 2005; Kharlamov 2012; Matsui 2015), Standard Mandarin (Kuo et al. 2007; Peng 2000; Xu 1993, 1997) and Taiwan Southern Min (Myers and Tsay 2008).

Although the empirical arguments for the phenomenon of incomplete neutralisation have been presented repeatedly, there has been a lingering suspicion that the observed phenomenon might be due to performance factors or simply task effects (Dinnsen and Charles-Luce 1984; Du and Durvasula 2022; Fourakis and Iverson 1984; Manaster Ramer 1996; Warner et al. 2004, amongst other). For example, many have pointed out that in such tasks, typically, the participant is given minimal pairs, which allows the participant to figure out the focus of the task and thereby produce somewhat unnatural/stylised speech (Fourakis and Iverson 1984; Roettger et al. 2014). In a recent study, Roettger et al. (2014) found a very small (non-significant) difference of about 2ms in vowel duration of the vowel preceding devoiced and underlyingly voiceless word-final stops in German, when they ran a controlled experiment that prevented the possibility of participants contrasting the stimuli or emulating patterns in the auditory input they received (Experiment 3 in Roettger et al. (2014)). However, in other conditions, they found a larger (significant) effect size. This suggests that task effects do need to be controlled for better in such experiments. Consequently, meta-analyses that include studies that have such confounds (Nicenboim et al. 2018) do not clearly tell us about the true nature of incomplete neutralisation, as they contain experimental protocols that aren't valid probes of the underlying constructs.

A second task effect that has been carefully inspected is that of orthography (Fourakis and Iverson 1984; Manaster Ramer 1996; Warner et al. 2004, amongst other). It has been noticed that in many previous studies, including the seminal work of Port and O'Dell (1985), the stimuli were presented orthographically. Since the contrast exists in the orthography, the participants may mirror the orthography and produce a slightly unnatural speech production pattern, thereby accounting for the observed differences. In fact, Warner et al. (2004) show exactly this possibility to be true in Dutch for pairs of words that are distinguished only orthographically, and don't have a phonological contrast as evidenced in the phonological patterning of those words.

In our opinion, one excellent piece of evidence that the phenomenon exists beyond orthographic effects comes from languages that use Chinese characters in their orthographic system. Although most Chinese characters were originally created with a sound part (J. Yang 2015), this connection was gradually lost due to historical sound changes and character modifications (Huang and Liao 2017). Researchers have observed incomplete neutralisation while employing Chinese characters to present the stimuli to the participants in different languages: Standard Mandarin (Kuo et al. 2007; Peng 2000; Xu 1993, 1997), Taiwan Southern Min (Myers and Tsay 2008), Huai'an Mandarin (Huai'an hereafter) (Du and Durvasula 2022), and Japanese (Braver and Kawahara 2016).

To take Standard Mandarin as an example, the crucial Tone 3 sandhi process states that a Tone 3 syllable becomes Tone 2 when immediately followed by another Tone 3 syllable. A rule-based mapping of the relevant phonological process is shown in (4) (Chen 2000; Cheng 2011; Duanmu 2007; Mei 1977).

4. Tone Sandhi in Standard Mandarin
    Tone 3 sandhi: T3 + T3 → T2 + T3

Despite the putative complete neutralisation in phonological representations, derived Tone 2 from Tone 3 has been shown to be phonetically different from underlying Tone 2 that has not undergone any phonological processes (Kuo et al. 2007; Peng 2000; Xu 1993, 1997). The phonetic difference is small but significant.

It is also worth commenting more on the study on Japanese. First, Chinese characters are very common in the Japanese writing system, and most of the stimuli in Braver and Kawahara's (2016) study were presented in Chinese characters (Kanji). Second, the connection between the sound part and pronunciation is even weaker in Japanese than that in Chinese languages. In Japanese, most Chinese characters have multiple pronunciations, *onyomi* and *kunyomi* (Itô and Mester 1999; Japan Broadcasting Corporation 1998). So, it is even harder to imagine the influence from orthography in Braver and Kawahara's study.

To sum up, despite worries about the ecological validity of the phenomenon, there are some clear cases of incomplete neutralisation that are unlikely to be caused by task effects rooted in experimental designs (or orthographic confounds).

2.1 The Issue of Phonological Neutralisation versus Phonetic Implementation

It is important to note that claims of incomplete neutralisation typically *assume* that the phonological contrast is phonologically neutralised in the case of the observed pattern at hand, and then show that there are (subtle) differences in the phonetics, hence the name of the phenomenon. However, many previous studies of incomplete neutralisation do not typically provide evidence that the examined process actually involves a phonological change. This part of the argument is crucial yet rarely addressed directly: if there is no phonological neutralisation with respect to the phenomenon under discussion in the first place, then there is no point in asking if there is incomplete phonetic neutralisation. Previous phonetic researchers exploring the phenomenon of incomplete neutralisation have simply *accepted* the analytic statements of phonologists; however, showing phonetically incomplete neutralisation in such a case, at best, falsifies the proposed analysis/claim, and not the overall framework of abstract representations; in fact, it doesn't even falsify the specific theory of representations used by the phonologist who proposed the specific analysis. So, one needs to show some independent evidence that there is indeed complete neutralisation in the phonology before testing the phenomenon of incomplete neutralisation.

One important attempt to establish phonologically complete neutralisation comes from Braver and Kawahara's (2016) production experiment on Japanese that we have mentioned. They creatively used the generalisation that a prosodic word almost always contains two moras on the surface in Japanese (Ito and Mester 2003; Itô 1990; Mori 2002; Poser 1990). The evidence for this generalisation mainly comes from processes where monosyllabic prosodic words are avoided. These processes include word-formation patterns, nickname formation, geisha-client name formation, loanword abbreviation, verbal root reduplication, scheduling compounds and telephone number recitation. To take the nickname formation process as an example – a full name is truncated to at least two moras long and then a suffix '-chan' is added as shown in (5). The name Wasaburoo and Kotomi are each truncated to be at least two moras long, which suggests a shortened form consisting of only one mora is likely ungrammatical.

5. Nickname Formation Process in Japanese (Data from Braver (2019))
    (a) Wasaburoo (full name)
        Wasa(-chan) (2 moras)
        *Wa(-chan) (1 mora)
    (b) Kotomi (full name)
        Koto(-chan) (2 moras)
        Koc(-chan) (2 moras)
        *Ko(-chan) (1 mora)

Based on such patterns, Braver and Kawahara (2016) suggest that, in order to be able to surface, an underlying monomoraic word has to lengthen to be bimoraic. Crucially, they observed that putatively lengthened bimoraic words have shorter durations than underlying bimoraic words. A potential issue with this argument 'however' is that this is at best indirect evidence for the lengthening process – one could have argued that the underlyingly monomoraic cases they looked at form exceptions to the otherwise regular generalisation. Note, this is no different from the fact that there are a variety of exceptions to the English pluralisation process, despite there being a regular process. See C. Yang (2016, and citations within) for multiple case studies on regular morphological processes in the face of exceptions.

Another attempt comes from a previous study of ours on Huai'an that we mentioned in the previous discussion (Du and Durvasula 2022). Here phonological behaviour was also employed to establish phonologically complete neutralisation. In this particular case, a feeding order between two phonological processes, one of which is the target process, is used to establish that the phonological process has indeed applied. We refer to the two phonological processes involved in the feeding order as *Target Process* and *Phonological Process 2*. If the *Target Process* results in a representation needed for the application of *Phonological Process 2* in a particular instance, and there is evidence in the pronunciation that the latter (*Phonological Process 2*) has applied, then we have evidence that the *Target Process* has applied. We can now check if the output of the *Target Process* is phonetically neutralising or not. In

Du and Durvasula (2022), we used this argument form to establish that a phonologically neutralising process of Tone 3 sandhi is phonetically non-neutralising. Based on the result, we argued that phonetic non-neutralisation is not a diagnostic of phonological non-neutralisation, and therefore should not count as an argument against abstract/discrete representations.

In this Element, we follow up on this research and present a new experiment that allows us to better understand the different non-phonological sources of incomplete neutralisation. Given that the experiments in this Element form a continuation of previous work, it is helpful to the reader, in our opinion, to both have a clear understanding of the relevant patterns in Huai'an, which will be the focus language for the experiment, and know the relevant data from Du and Durvasula (2022). For this reason, in Section 2.2.1, we will provide the basic information and relevant phonological processes in Huai'an. We will then discuss, in Section 2.2.2, the previous experimental studies on Huai'an, which show that Huai'an has a clear case of incomplete neutralisation. Next, in Section 2.3, we will list the requirements that any explanations on incomplete neutralisation should meet. Based on these requirements, we will point out the problems with previous accounts in Section 2.4, and then provide our own new explanation in Section 3. In Section 4, we will introduce the new experiment we conducted, which provides experimental evidence for our theory.

2.2 Evidence from Huai'an Mandarin

2.2.1 Background on Huai'an Mandarin

Huai'an is a Mandarin language that belongs to Jianghuai Guanhua Group (Lower Yangtze Mandarin). The native speakers of the language are mainly from and currently reside in Huai'an city, which is located about 210 miles (340 kilometers) north of Shanghai (Wang and Kang 1989). Huai'an has four phonemic tones. In accordance with the tradition of describing Mandarin languages (Chao 1930), the four tones are referred to as Tone 1, Tone 2, Tone 3, and Tone 4 (Jiao 2004; Wang and Kang 2012). In Table 1, the four tones are given with tonal letters on a scale of 1 to 5 where 1 is the lowest f0 and 5 is the highest f0 (Chao 1930). The tonal contours of tones (in isolation) are illustrated in Figure 1.

The three tone sandhi processes that are involved in Du and Durvasula (2022) are shown in (6). These processes are also used in the new experiment that we will present in this Element. In the stimuli, each syllable forms a separate word, therefore the tone sandhi processes in the stimuli only occur at the post-lexical level. At the post-lexical level, the low-register Tone 3 sandhi is mandatory when the syllable that undergoes tone sandhi and the syllable that

Table 1 Tonemes in Huai'an Mandarin

Phonemic Tones	Tone Letter	Contour Description
Tone 1 (T1)	42	high falling
Tone 2 (T2)	24	high rising
Tone 3 (T3)	212	low/low rising
Tone 4 (T4)	55	high level

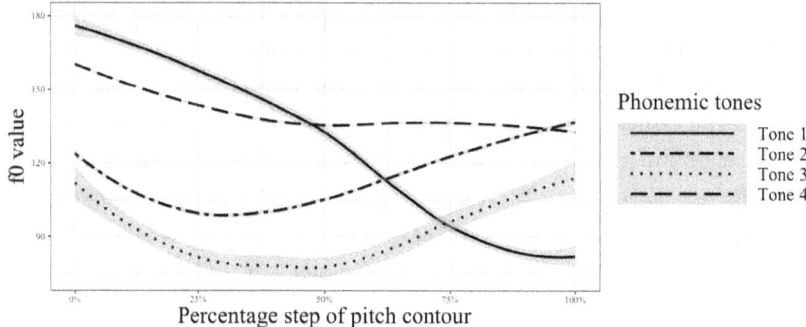

Figure 1 Tonal contour of phonemic tones in Huai'an

triggers tone sandhi are in the same phonological phrase. And Tone 3 sandhi becomes optional when the two syllables involved are not required to be in the same phonological phrase. In contrast, the high-register Tone 1 and Tone 4 sandhis are always optional and in fact only applicable when the two syllables involved belong to the same phonological phrase.[21]

Tone 3 sandhi in Huai'an is highly similar to that in Standard Mandarin as shown in (4). Here in Huai'an, a Tone 3 syllable becomes Tone 2 when triggered by another Tone 3 syllable. It is worth noting that Tone 3 can be either underlying or derived to trigger the Tone 3 sandhi process.

---

[21] We recognise that there are multiple potential sources of optionality/variability. As we will discuss later, some optionality can be attributed to planning effects, and some optionality is likely from multiple grammars that a speaker has knowledge of (diglossia), and some is from within the same grammar either due to optional processes or multiple representations. Given that the sentential structures we use are the same for all the tone sandhi cases in the current study, it is difficult to attribute the differential optionality of the processes to planning. However, it can stem from either multiple grammars or from variation within the same grammar. Furthermore, as we will point out in the last paragraph of Section 2.2.1, we followed the conservative view and only analysed the derived Tone 3 tokens that actually trigger Tone 3 sandhi in both Du and Durvasula (2022) and in the current experiment reported in this Element. So, optionality is used to set up the contrasts for comparison.

6. Tone Sandhi in Huai'an Mandarin
   (a) Low register Tone Sandhi
       Tone 3 sandhi: T3 + T3 → T2 + T3
   (b) High register Tone Sandhi
       Tone 1 sandhi: T1 + T1 → T3 + T1
       Tone 4 sandhi: T4 + T4 → T3 + T4

Crucially, the Tone 3 output of the high-register tone sandhi processes in (6b) feeds the low-register Tone 3 sandhi process in (6a) as exemplified in (7). Since both high-register tone and Tone 3 sandhi are optional given different possible prosodic structures for utterances in (7), multiple surface representations are possible.

7. Feeding order in Huai'an Mandarin (boldface and underline represent the locus of a potential feeding order application due to a relevant tone sandhi process; the data is from Du and Durvasula (2022))

   (a) Tone 1 sandhi feeds Tone 3 sandhi
       u   ku   fən
       Mr. Wu   estimate   score
       'Mr. Wu estimate score'.

UR	T3 T1 T1		
Tone 1 sandhi	T3 T3 T1	(or)	T3 T1 T1
Tone 3 sandhi	T2 T3 T1 (or) T3 T3 T1		T3 T1 T1
SR	**T2 T3 T1** (or) T3 T3 T1		T3 T1 T1

   (b) Tone 4 sandhi feeds Tone 3 sandhi
       u   to   ə
       Mr. Wu   chop   meat
       'Mr. Wu chops meat'.

UR	T3 T4 T4		
Tone 4 sandhi	T3 T3 T4	(or)	T3 T4 T4
Tone 3 sandhi	T2 T3 T4 (or) T3 T3 T4		T3 T4 T4
SR	**T2 T3 T4** (or) T3 T3 T4		T3 T4 T4

Based on the feeding relationships and the logic we have stated in Section 2.1, we suggest that the high-register tone sandhis results in a Tone 3 category that is phonologically the same as an underlying Tone 3. Given that Tone 4 and

Tone 1 sandhi processes are optional, one should be more conservative and look at only those instances where the outputs of Tone 4 or Tone 1 sandhi processes in turn trigger Tone 3 sandhi, as such a feeding interaction would suggest that Tone 4 or Tone 1 sandhi did result in a tone that is phonologically identical with the underlying Tone 3, since they share the same unique phonological behaviour in Huai'an, namely triggering Tone 3 sandhi.

In order to be rigorous, in Du and Durvasula (2022), we followed the conservative view and only analysed the derived Tone 3 tokens that actually triggered Tone 3 sandhi in their article. The crucial surface representations under analysis are underlined and boldfaced in (7).

2.2.2 Previous Experimental Results on Huai'an Mandarin

We first present the data for Tone 1 sandhi in Du and Durvasula (2022). The z-score transformed f0 contours on the crucial second syllable are shown in Figure 2. As a reminder, the crucial comparison is between a derived Tone 3 and an underlying Tone 3, where both tones are after derived Tone 2s and therefore in the same surface context – the feeding relationship establishes that both the Tone 3s are categorically Tone 3 as they trigger Tone 3 sandhi. The tone contour for an underlying Tone 1 is also presented in the same surface context for visual comparison with the two crucial Tone 3s.

Based on the visual inspection of the data, the derived Tone 3 seems to start as an underlying Tone 3 and ends as an underlying Tone 1. And the contour shape of the derived Tone 3 is close to that of an underlying Tone 3. Furthermore, the comparison between underlying Tone 3 and derived Tone 3 clearly shows that the neutralisation is incomplete and has a large unstandardised effect size. The average difference is 18 Hz and the maximum difference is 32 Hz.

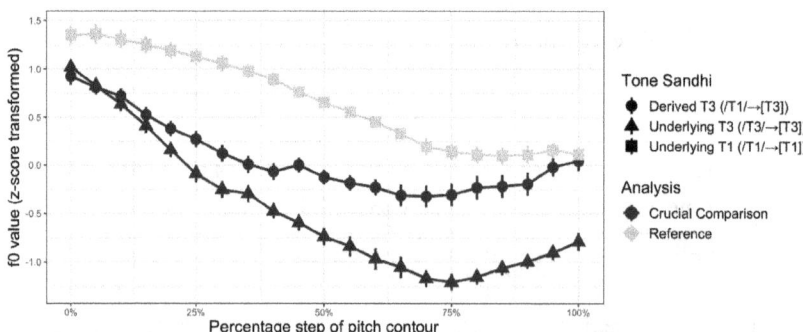

Figure 2 Contours comparison of the second syllable in Du and Durvasula's experiment (Tone 1 sandhi) (Error bars indicate standard error)

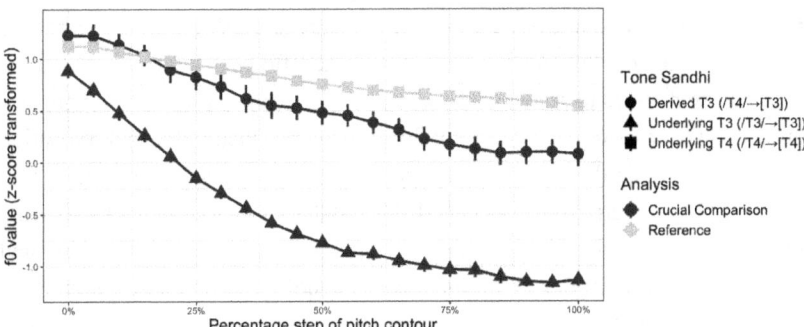

Figure 3 Contours comparison of the second syllable in Du and Durvasula's experiment (Tone 4 sandhi) (Error bars indicate standard error)

Similarly, for Tone 4 sandhi, the z-score transformed f0 contours on the crucial second syllable are shown in Figure 3. Again, the crucial comparison is between a derived Tone 3 and an underlying Tone 3, where both tones are after derived Tone 2s and therefore in the same surface context. Similar to Tone 1 sandhi, the tone contour for an underlying Tone 4 is also presented in the same surface context for visual comparison with the two crucial Tone 3s. Based on visual inspection of the data, the pattern seems to be different from the case of Tone 1 sandhi. The derived Tone 3 seems to start as an underlying Tone 4, instead of as an underlying Tone 3 as in the experiment for Tone 1 sandhi. Furthermore, the derived Tone 3 gradually deviates from underlying Tone 4 through the whole contour; note, this is in contrast to the case of Tone 1 sandhi, where the derived Tone 3 ended up at a value almost identical to the underlying Tone 1. However, the contour shape of the derived Tone 3 is again close to that of an underlying Tone 3 as in Tone 1 sandhi. Despite the difference, incomplete phonetic neutralisation is again clearly observed with a substantial unstandardised effect size in the comparison between underlying Tone 3 and derived Tone 3. The average difference is 17 Hz and the maximum difference is 27 Hz.

In both cases, subsequent statistical modelling using Growth Curve Analysis supported the observations made in the visual inspection. We have not included the statistical modelling in terms of Growth Curve Analysis here in the interest of concision, but refer the readers to Du and Durvasula (2022) for further discussion. Note further, that we present similar statistical modelling for the new data following for the reader to get a better idea of the modelling technique.

2.3 Desiderata for Any Explanation for Incomplete Neutralisation

It is worth reminding the reader that, as we have discussed in the beginning of Section 2, incomplete neutralisation cases with a small effect size have incurred many criticisms about task demands. If orthographic effects or task demands are the ultimate causal source for the measured difference in production, there is of course no need to provide any other linguistic explanation of the phenomenon. However, as we have stated in Section 2, some incomplete neutralisation patterns in Standard Mandarin (Kuo et al. 2007; Peng 2000; Xu 1993, 1997) and Taiwan Southern Min (Myers and Tsay 2008) have a small effect size while being immune to the influence of orthography, since the stimuli are presented in Chinese characters that are remote from phonological/phonetic qualities.

Another notable criticism comes from the interpretation of the results. Such a small effect size has been argued to likely not be functionally significant and therefore is not in need of a linguistic explanation (Dinnsen and Charles-Luce 1984; Mascaró 1987; Warner et al. 2004). From the point of view of native speakers, they may not be able to distinguish phonological categories using such a small phonetic difference and therefore are likely to analyse them to be in the same category in phonology anyway. In fact, some previous studies on incomplete neutralisation have shown that phonetic differences are still perceptually distinguishable (Port and O'Dell 1985; Warner et al. 2004, amongst others). However, since stimuli in the elicitation task always contain the minimal pairs in these studies, unnatural speech may be brought out where the contrast between derived form and its underlying counterpart is exaggerated. And such unnatural speech may be the reason why native speakers can distinguish phonological categories in the following perceptual task.

To be consistent with the previous literature, we still treat incomplete neutralisation cases with small effect sizes as incomplete neutralisation despite the criticism we discussed earlier. By doing so, we also assume that the contrast is indeed neutralised phonologically although previous studies do not typically provide evidence as stated in Section 2.1. Based on this, we continue to use the term 'incomplete neutralisation with a small effect size'. We employ *Just Noticeable Difference* (Weber 1905) as the yardstick to assign phenomena as having small versus large effect sizes. Henceforth, an incomplete neutralisation with an effect size that is smaller than the corresponding *Just Noticeable Difference* (JND) will be called 'incomplete neutralisation with a small effect size'. In contrast, an incomplete neutralisation with an effect size that is larger than the corresponding JND will be called 'incomplete neutralisation with a large effect size'. We realise that using JNDs as a metric for effect sizes is a somewhat crude technique (to assign functional importance). However, given the current state of knowledge, we aren't aware of a better metric. Having said that, this is an avenue of research that is worth pursuing on its own in the future.

Quite naturally, the next question to ask is: How does one explain the phenomenon? Why exactly do phonologically identical surface forms have different phonetic distributions? Before we discuss extant theories of incomplete neutralisation, we would like to lay out the desiderata as stated in Du and Durvasula (2022), and connect the discussion to the broader issues raised in Section 1. These desiderata, in our opinion, serve as necessary requirements for any theory that attempts to explain the phenomenon of incomplete neutralisation specifically, and the gap between phonetics and phonology more generally. As will be seen, crucial to the desiderata is the distinction between *explanatory* and *non-explanatory* accounts that we elaborated on in Section 1.

In the following section (Section 2.4), we will use the desiderata as a lens to understand the effectiveness of previous theories. And, in Section 3, we will present a new explanation that is entirely consistent with both the desiderata and the *classic generative phonology* view, which locates the source of the issue to be in planning, and actually outside the phonology proper.

8. Desiderata for a theory of incomplete neutralisation
    (a) The simplest account of why incomplete neutralisation exists as a phenomenon.
    (b) An *explanation* for the actual distribution of effect sizes among different phonological processes.
    (c) An *explanation* of why 'over-neutralisation' is never observed.
    (d) An *explanation* of how a feeding interaction is possible with another phonological process if there is phonetically incomplete neutralisation.
    (e) Related to 8d, an *explanation* of why incompletely neutralised segments can trigger another phonological process (referred to as *Phonological Process 2*), but other phonetically similar segments do not.

First, according to the Law of Parsimony (Occam's Razor), the simplest explanation should be prioritised (8a). Therefore, if incomplete neutralisation can be explained using independently needed performance factors, there is no need to further complicate phonology or lexical representations. Beyond previously identified factors such as orthography and task effects, performance factors that need to be explored further include phonological planning (Kilbourn-Ceron and Goldrick 2021; Tanner et al. 2017; M. Wagner 2012), cascaded activation of morphemes during production (Goldrick and Blumstein 2006), and the variability of phonological processes.[22] We will suggest later in

---

[22] In Du and Durvasula (2022), we suggested that the variability in the different rates of tone sandhi application with derived and underlying Tone 3 could themselves be reduced to a different planning effect. However, the proposals related to phonological planning are largely about planning words/morphemes, so it would be an extrapolation of our previous claim to include intra-morpheme variability or socio-phonological variability as being part of it; therefore, one

this Element that these sources can indeed be some of the causes for incomplete neutralisation. In our opinion, in light of these possibilities, complicating and elaborating phonological representations (or phonological knowledge more generally) is currently both unnecessary and unjustified.

The second challenge facing theories of incomplete neutralisation is the systematic disparity in effect sizes (8b). The proposed theory of incomplete neutralisation should explain not only cases with big effect sizes such as Huai'an tone sandhis, but also previous cases with small effect sizes such as devoicing in German, Polish, Catalan, for example. Note here, we want to bring back the distinction between explanation and non-explanatory accounts that we laid out earlier. As mentioned, crucial to the distinction is that if a theory is truly an explanation of a phenomenon, then the theory will *entail* the phenomenon (all things being equal), or in probabilistic terms the theory will make the phenomenon much more likely than the absence/converse of the phenomenon (all things being equal). That is, a theory is *explanatory* to the extent that it predicts reality (but not its converse/absence). If on the other hand, a theory can simply account for reality but can also accommodate the absence/converse of reality, then it is at best a non-explanatory account, that is, it is a redescription of the phenomenon (see Cummins 2000, for relevant discussion). For our purposes, any theory of incomplete neutralisation that can *account* for a small effect size for devoicing but can also account for a large effect size of incomplete devoicing, without further clarifying under what circumstances one can see the former and not the latter and vice versa, is simply a redescription of the observed data, not an explanation of the observed phenomena.

Related to the second challenge, and expanding on the crucial distinction between simple re-descriptions and true explanations, the third challenge is that the proposed explanation should not only predict the existence of cases of 'incomplete neutralisation', but also predict the general absence of 'over-neutralisation', defined as the degree of application being beyond the phonetic distribution of the target underlying category (8c). Back to the case of German devoicing, under the scenario of 'incomplete neutralisation', the phonetic cues of derived voiceless stops fall between underlying voiceless stops and underlying voiced stops. While under the scenario of 'over-neutralisation', the

---

should not interpret our previous claim as extending to *all* socio-phonological variation. Furthermore, more relevant to this Element is the issue that such proposals cannot readily explain why the same syntactic structures should result in different rates of application for different tone sandhi processes (Tone 1 and Tone 4 sandhis in Huai'an). While being a logical possibility (which is an extremely weak criterion), it would be a leap of faith to suggest that all variability should be reduced to planning without a concrete proposal to explain the specific patterns.

phonetic cues of underlying voiceless stops fall between derived voiceless stops and underlying voiced stops. However, only 'incomplete neutralisation' has been observed.

The fourth challenge that any theory of incomplete neutralisation faces is explaining the possibility of a feeding interaction – Why can a derived form that is phonetically incomplete still trigger another phonological process just like a phonetically complete form (8d)? For example, in the case of Huai'an, the Tone 3 output of the high-register tone sandhi processes can feed the low-register Tone 3 sandhi process as in (7) despite incompletely neutralising with underlying Tone 3 in the phonetics. As we pointed out in Du and Durvasula (2022), any abstract/discrete theory of phonological representations naturally accounts for this in terms of categorical rule/process interactions. Of course, it is logically possible for a gradient phonological representation to do so too; however, without specific claims about what the permissible computations and representations are, we are at best back to claiming something rather weak, namely, logical possibility/consistency, which we showed is even weaker in the case of high-dimensional and gradient representations.

The final challenge that any theory of incomplete neutralisation faces is explaining why phonetically incompletely neutralised segments can trigger a feeding process, but other phonetically similar segments do not (8d). This challenge is particularly problematic for high-dimensional and gradient representations. Of course, given that (very) high-dimensionality and gradience, it is quite easy to say that there might be some difference between the two cases. However, the challenge is to propose a specific set of high-dimensional and gradient representations that are testable beyond the data at hand – therefore the challenge is in not just accounting for the observed patterns, but actually *explaining* why it happens.

2.4 Previous Accounts for Incomplete Neutralisation

Recall at the beginning of Section 2 we stated that the definition of incomplete neutralisation is twofold and involves both the phonology and the phonetics. A neutralisation process should be classified as 'incomplete neutralisation' only when it has been argued to be complete in the phonology but incomplete in the phonetics. Therefore, the account of incomplete neutralisation can logically lie in the phonological representations, or their manifestations in phonetics, or the interface between phonological representations and the phonetics. It turns out proposals have been made in all three of these domains. For this section, we will discuss previous accounts of incomplete neutralisation and point out their problems based on the desiderata stated in Section 2.3.

2.4.1 Accounts That Modify Phonological Representations

The accounts that use phonological representations to model incomplete neutralisation generally introduce gradience into phonological representations (McCollum 2019; Port and Leary 2005; Roettger et al. 2014, amongst others). Under such a framework, the assumption of abstract/discrete phonological representations is dropped, and high-dimensional gradient representations are proposed. A consensus has not been reached by previous studies on exactly how to incorporate gradience inside formal phonology (Lionnet 2017; Pierrehumbert et al. 2000; Silverman 2006; Tucker and Warner 2010), but McCollum (2019) argues that some form of continuously valued variables has to be employed in order to do so. To apply this perspective to German final devoicing, phonology should not only instruct an underlyingly voiced segment to devoice, but also represent to what degree the devoicing process should occur to distinguish the derived voiceless segment from its underlying counterpart. We note here that one could equally have simply extended the range of discrete/abstract features as we alluded to earlier in Section 1.5, and this would result in a far smaller lexical hypothesis space than with high-dimensional gradient representations. But this option has not, to our knowledge, been explored.

Despite the fact that the observed effect of incomplete neutralisation can be straightforwardly accounted for by incorporating gradience into phonological representations, the proposed new theory also becomes much weaker and predicts many more possible grammars. To appreciate this statement, under the *classic generative phonology* view, only very few grammars are possible for the final obstruent devoicing process like that in German: one grammar in which [+voice] feature (or equivalent) in the underlying representation is deleted and is replaced by [-voice] feature in the surface representation, a second grammar in which [+voice] feature is delinked without being replaced by [-voice] feature (Wiese 2000), and a third possibility in which [+spread glottis] feature is inserted in the surface representation, and a few other similar variants involving other laryngeal features (such as [constricted glottis]).

In contrast, under the proposed new theory of gradient phonological representations, an infinite set of grammars is possible, differing in the degree to which the devoicing happens.

The second issue with introducing gradience into phonological representations is that it does not offer a satisfying explanation for the systematic disparity in effect sizes as stated in (8b). If an infinite set of grammars is available with a varying range of effect size possibilities and are presumably equiprobable, then we can't explain why the actual phenomenon has the effect size that it does. The third issue is that this framework can potentially predict cases of 'over-neutralisation' as stated in (8c). However, only 'incomplete neutralisation' has been observed in previously examined languages, which is in contrast with this prediction. The last issue, as discussed under (8d–8e), is that such a framework cannot offer a satisfying explanation for how a feeding interaction is possible under the condition of incomplete phonetic neutralisation.[23]

Again, these issues are particularly problematic for any purely high-dimensional gradient (exemplar) representations (Brown and McNeill 1966; Bybee 1994; Goldinger 1996, 1997; Port and Leary 2005; Roettger et al. 2014) and hybrid representational models (Pierrehumbert 2002, 2016). Based on the criteria we have laid out in (8), we suggest that such theories are typically redescriptions of the phenomenon without providing an explanation for the phenomenon.

It is also worth noting here that, as pointed out by an anonymous reviewer, incomplete neutralisation can potentially be accounted for by assuming the existence of multiple grammars that conform to the *classic generative phonology* view. Again, to take German as an example. It is possible that different speakers have different grammars. Perhaps one grammar states that [+voice] feature is replaced by [-voice] feature; in other words, /d/ becomes [t] in the surface representation. The other grammar states that [+voice] feature is delinked without being replaced by [-voice] feature (Wiese 2000); in other words, /d/ becomes [D] in the surface representation. Under such an account, when the mean of some phonetic measurement for underlying /d/ (that can surface as both [t] and [D]) is compared with underlying /t/ (that can only surface as [t]), there would be a difference due to an averaging artefact across speakers. Overall, such an account conforms to the *classic generative phonology* view. However, no phonetic evidence supports this account to the best of the authors' knowledge. In German, under the multiple grammars account, phonetic distributions of /t/ in a prosodic-word final context should be unimodal, but those for /d/ in the same prosodic-word final context should be bimodal; however, no previous studies have observed this (Port and O'Dell 1985; Roettger et al. 2014). Similarly, no multimodal distributions have been reported in other cases of incomplete neutralisation (Braver and Kawahara 2016; Du and Durvasula 2022; Warner et al. 2004, amongst others).

---

[23] The one exception to this is McCollum (2019), who actually proposes simultaneously discrete and gradient representations in order to account for patterns in Uyghur. However, in recent collaborative work with McCollum, the second author has argued the crucial pattern of gradience observed in Uyghur stems from improper control of segmental/morphological contexts (McCollum et al. 2023).

2.4.2 Accounts in the Phonology–Phonetics Interface

The accounts aiming to revise the phonology–phonetics interface generally involve revising what phonetics can see inside phonology. As noticed by many previous researchers, the direction of incomplete neutralisation is almost always towards the underlying representation before derivation (Gouskova and Hall 2009; Van Oostendorp 2008). Again to take the German devoicing case as an example, all examined phonetic cues of derived voiceless stops deviate from underlying voiceless stops and manifest closer to underlying voiced stops. In light of this, the proposal has been made that both underlying representation and surface representation should be available for phonetic manifestations. An incompletely neutralised form is then generated by blending these two representations (Gafos and Benus 2006; Nelson and Heinz 2021; Van Oostendorp 2008, amongst others).

The virtue of such an analysis of blending (underlying and surface) representations is that it traps the incomplete neutralisation in-between two representations, namely the underlying and surface representations. So, in a case like German devoicing, a devoiced voiced stop is predicted to be in-between a voiced stop and a voiceless stop in its phonetic manifestation. This guarantees an explanation for why 'over-neutralisation' never happens.

There is, however, one big issue with this general viewpoint. In the absence of further restrictions/constraints, it does not offer a satisfying explanation for the systematic disparity in effect sizes as stated in (8b). Furthermore, similar to accounts that modify phonological representations, with no constraints on the degree of influence from underlying representations, the produced sound can fall at any point on the spectrum between underlying and surface representations – so, we should in fact find a range of languages with a uniform distribution of neutralisation effects. This is again contrary to the observed facts. Of course, one could stipulate that surface representations are more important for phonetic manifestations (Nelson and Heinz 2021), but such a stipulation is just that, a stipulation, and furthermore it would be at best a redescription of the facts, as it doesn't really clarify why surface representations are more important than underlying representations if both of them are accessible to the phonetics. Later, we ourselves suggest a version of this general analysis strategy that sidesteps the issues discussed in this paragraph by appealing to planning factors.

2.4.3 Accounts from Phonetics

Finally, Braver (2019) proposed an account that we suggest falls in the realm of phonetics with the model of Weighted Phonetic Constraint

(Flemming 2001). Under such a constraint-based framework that is similar to Optimality Theory (Prince and Smolensky 1993/2004), the phonetic details are no longer just a consequence of Universal Phonetics (Chomsky and Halle 1968; Volenec and Reiss 2017). Therefore, phonetic values are not automatically decided or determined but can be different under the same phonetic context for the same piece of information transferred from phonology. One possible way in which to flesh this out is by following up on what Flemming (2001) proposed: namely, that the actual phonetic value is computed by a compromise among a series of weighted constraints. Utilising this perspective, Braver (2019) accounted for the incomplete neutralisation in Japanese (discussed in Section 2.1) as a paradigm uniformity effect in the phonetics where a related morphological base can affect the phonetic manifestation of the word, akin to the paradigm uniformity effects that have been argued in phonological patterns (Benua 1995; Burzio 1994, 1998; Flemming 1995; Kenstowicz 1995; Kiparsky 1978; Yu 2007). Recall in Section 2.1, as suggested by Braver and Kawahara (2016), an underlying monomoraic word has to be lengthened to be bimoraic in order to surface in Japanese. In phonetics, such a markedness constraint is formalised by Braver (2019) as a phonetic duration target for bimoraic words: TARGETDUR($\mu\mu$), while paradigm uniformity effect requires bimoraic words to be faithful to its monomorabic base: OO-ID(dur). With the interaction of these two constraints, the phonetic value of the output fall between an underlying monomoraic word and an underlying bimoraic word.

Similar to high-dimensional and gradient representations, the theory doesn't explain the actual distribution of effect sizes (8b). However, as with the blending view, it potentially prevents 'over-neutralisation' (8c). But this is so only to the extent that the relevant base is phonologically similar to the actual word under consideration; consequently, the theory doesn't necessarily prevent 'over-neutralisation' even for the standard cases.

Finally, it is not at all clear that a separate phonetic grammar is even necessary (8a). In the literature, two main motivations have been provided for assuming there is a phonetic grammar along with a phonological grammar. First, by doing so, one can account for language-specific variation that is typically seen to be a problem for abstract/discrete phonological representations (Keating 1985). However, we'd like to point out the important discussions in Hale et al. (2007) and Volenec and Reiss (2017), which highlight that there is no such issue at all. One can easily imagine different combinations of abstract phonological representations leading to different phonetic manifestations in different languages. To take Mandarin languages as an example, Tone 1 in Standard Mandarin is a high level tone, while in Huai'an it is pronounced as a high falling tone (Chao 1930; Jiao 2004; Wang and Kang 2012). Such differences are commonly assigned to a difference in phonological representations (Woo 1969): Tone 1 in Standard Mandarin can be represented as two high tonal targets in high register, while Tone 1 in Huai'an can be represented as a high tonal target plus a low tonal target in high register. In this way, the difference in phonetics does not need to be attributed to language-specific phonetics, but simply to different phonological representations.

A second motivation provided by Flemming (2001) is that there seem to be many parallels between phonetics and phonology, and such parallels could be interpreted as suggesting that phonetics and phonology operate with similar mechanisms and may be treated in a unified framework. An example that is relevant to incomplete neutralisation is assimilation and coarticulation. However, here too, such a view presupposes what it has to show/argue for. One can again easily imagine that all observed coarticulation is simply a manifestation of different abstract phonological representations and computations in different languages. In fact, this issue has been explicitly discussed by quite a few in the past (Hale et al. 2007; Hammarberg 1976, 1982; Volenec and Reiss 2017), but the relevant discussion has, as far as we can see, simply been ignored (we don't imply intentionality here) by those arguing for language-specific phonetic grammars/knowledge.[24]

With the previous discussion, it should be clear to the reader that we are actually suggesting that there is not enough clear dispositive evidence to propose a separate language-specific phonetic grammar module despite the popularity of the view in current laboratory phonology research. Furthermore, we'd like to point out that lurking underneath the discussion is an opinion that any level of consistency with a framework is sufficient, and again we'd like to point out that this is a rather weak requirement.

3 Our Explanation for Incomplete Neutralisation

Before we delve into the specifics of our explanation, given our discussion in Section 1, it is worth reiterating that there is no tension between the claims of

---

[24] A reviewer asks if the *common strawman view of discrete representations* entails language-specific phonetics. This will depend on other auxiliary assumptions, so there is no clear cut answer to the question. If a language-specific phonetics module is allowed to neutralise distinctions in the categorical surface form, then the answer is no, as the auxiliary hypothesis in our opinion would violate the spirit of the *common strawman view of discrete representations*; and if language-specific phonetics is not allowed to neutralise such differences (through some mechanism), the the answer would be yes, as the auxiliary hypothesis would be consistent with the spirit of the *common strawman view of discrete representations*. In fact, Keating (1990) tacitly suggests the latter in her window model of coarticulation (although, the actual specifics of the model don't preclude the possibility of neutralisation). We ourselves take no position, so have remained neutral in the document.

classic generative phonology and incomplete neutralisation. As a reminder, the true claims of this view ride on an *all things being equal* clause. Specifically, the framework predicts that two representations with the same phonological content must have the same performance (phonetics) if all things are equal. However, in the case of incomplete neutralisation, by definition, all things aren't equal, since the derived representation and the underived representation have different underlying representations (or lexical representations). Now, one might argue this is unfair or unreasonable, but there is nothing unfair about the claim from a generative perspective. As far as we can see, the response seems unfair or unnatural only when the reader makes further assumptions beyond what is claimed as essential to the framework; that is, the reader in such cases is invoking additional auxiliary assumptions. For example, it seems to us if one makes the auxiliary assumption that only the derived surface representation matters (and not the underlying representation) for phonetic manifestations, one might be led to the conclusion that the rebuttal is unfair or unreasonable. But, the specific auxiliary assumption is what needs to be debated, as it is not entailed by *classic generative phonology*.[25]

To belabour the point even more, beyond the fact that a derived representation and an underived representation have different underlying representations (lexical representations), two lexical items being separate come with a host of other differences; for example, different word frequencies, potentially different parts of speech, and consequently different syntactic and prosodic structures. Given that the *all things being equal* clause is not satisfied, there is no inconsistency between the observation of incomplete neutralisation and the *classic generative phonology* view.

While the lack of inconsistency is a starting point, we don't believe such a state of affairs is sufficiently satisfactory as an *explanation* of the phenomenon (i.e., assuming one is interested in explaining the phenomenon, of course). To address this, we will show that even if one espouses a purely feedforward system such as *classic generative phonology*, wherein surface representations (and not underlying representations) are interpreted by the phonetics, with nuanced auxiliary hypotheses about phonological planning, one can still see the influence of the underlying representation indirectly. In what follows, we will flesh out the relevant auxiliary hypotheses.

For previously observed cases of incomplete neutralisation with a small effect size (e.g. final devoicing in German, Dutch, and Russian), we

---

[25] A close analogy can be drawn between this case and cases where two sentences have the same syntactic structure but different lexical items – we don't deem it to be unfair to claim that the performance (say, the acceptability of the sentence) needn't be identical though the structures are identical. In fact, that is the very reason syntacticians standardly use very closely controlled sentences to probe syntactic knowledge.

suggest that the effect falls out of the independently needed performance factor of incremental phonological planning (Ferreira and Swets 2002; Kilbourn-Ceron and Goldrick 2021; Tanner et al. 2017; M. Wagner 2012). The claim offers an explanation without invoking any changes to the categorical phonological representations or knowledge or to other aspects. The central claim is that speakers incrementally plan out the phonological contents beyond the current morpheme or word. When this situation occurs and the phonological details of the next morpheme or word are not immediately available, the underlying representation of the current word will be planned as corresponding identical surface representations since the relevant environment is not present for the process to be triggered (provided no other phonological processes are relevant). As time transpires during planning, when the phonological details of the next morpheme or word become available, the phonological process is applied during the planning and another surface representation is outputted based on the phonology and the representation can also be planned. Therefore, speakers can have a set of antagonistic planned surface representations for the same underlying representation at the same time. And the output in production will be a blend of a set of multiple planned surface representations. Finally, the effect of the more recently planned surface representations is stronger due to a recency bias (Glanzer and Cunitz 1966; Rundus 1971; Waugh and Norman 1965), so the output in production is predicted to be closer to the latter surface representation (i.e., the surface representation that is the result of the application of the phonological processes) – this results in a small effect size in incomplete neutralisation. Since the mechanism we propose for incomplete neutralisation with a large effect size may also be understood as a phonological planning effect, we use the term *incremental unitary planning effect* to refer to the mechanism introduced in this paragraph.

Let's take the German final devoicing as an example: when a morpheme with a final voiced stop is encountered in planning, the speaker doesn't know that the rule/process environment of prosodic word-finality is met. Therefore, they plan a morpheme final voiced stop. Further incremental processing allows the speaker to plan subsequent morphemes, and if the first morpheme does appear at the end of a prosodic word, then the devoicing process is planned. Consequently, the speaker has planned a set of surface representations for the same underlying representation at the same time, and a more recently planned voiceless obstruent will blend with a previously planned surfaced voiced obstruent, causing the output to be more voiced than an underlying voiceless obstruent and resulting in incomplete neutralisation. Furthermore, the effect of more recently planned voiceless obstruent is stronger due to a recency effect, so the output in production is predicted to be closer to a voiceless stop, which results in a small effect size in incomplete neutralisation.

Here, it is important to note that there are two different serial-position effects that have been identified in prior work on memory: recency bias and primacy bias (Glanzer and Cunitz 1966); the former results in more recent exposures being weighted higher and the latter results in initial exposures being weighted higher. If a primacy bias were to play a role in speech production, then our explanation that depends purely on a recency bias would become a redescription of the data. However, a careful look at the memory literature shows that recency effects and primacy effects have different signatures and have been argued to occur due to different memory systems. There is clear evidence of double dissociation between the two effects based on damage to different areas of the neocortex (Milner 1970; Vallar and Shallice 1990). Recency effects have been argued to be due to the nature of short-term memory and correlate with short-term memory loss. In contrast, primacy effects have been argued to be due to the nature of long-term memory and correlate with long-term memory loss (Rundus 1971; Waugh and Norman 1965) – such effects are often seen to be due to rehearsal of the input (which benefits earlier items the most), but see Greene et al. (2000) for a more recent review and modelling of these effects that argues against rehearsal as the mechanism for primacy effects. In our case of *incremental unitary planning effect*, we clearly intend the planned representations to be part of working memory during processing, which involves the use of short-term memory and not long-term memory (Baddeley 2000; Cowan 2008); that is, we make no claims that the multiple planned representations enter long-term memory, as there would be no theoretical justification for such planned representations to either be rehearsed or be part of long-term memory. Consequently, primacy effects should not play a role in incremental planning for production. Finally, based on these statements, our theory also makes a novel prediction that incomplete neutralisation with a small effect size should likely be attenuated further if working memory is impaired. However, this latter prediction is predicated on an assumption that tests used to measure general working memory in fact probe the working memory as used in speech production.

One might argue that the incremental nature of the planning we propose is new and *ad hoc*. However, as we pointed out earlier in this section, such a planning view is seen to be necessary for independent reasons (Ferreira and Swets 2002; Kilbourn-Ceron and Goldrick 2021; Tanner et al. 2017; M. Wagner 2012). Furthermore, perception has been argued to be incremental for a rather long time (see Norris and McQueen 2008, and citations within), so it would be rather surprising if production (being another performance output) were not incrementally planned too.[26]

Another prediction our view makes is that with more time for planning, the effect size of the incomplete neutralisation should decrease. This is so because there would be more planned representations where the process has applied, and therefore, the weighted effect of more recently planned representations should be stronger. One way to test this prediction concretely is by looking at slower speech rates. Under the assumption of there being more time for planning with slower speech rates and consequently a larger set of planned surface representations, we would predict that the effect size of incomplete neutralisation would decrease in slower speech rates (as compared to faster speech rates).

A further prediction is possible provided we make an assumption about how memory load interacts with short-term memory. For example, if a memory load were to effectively shorten the window of short-term memory (this can be cashed out in many different ways, of course), then one would predict that the size of the the incomplete neutralisation effect stemming from the *incremental unitary planning effect* would decrease. This is so because, if a memory load during speech production results in an effectively shorter short-term memory window, given the recency bias we mentioned earlier, it would disadvantage the older planned representations, and therefore the produced output would be even closer in form to the more recently planned outputs. For example, in the German word-final devoicing case, with a memory load, the set of planned surface representations would have fewer voiced consonants in a word-final position; consequently, the actual output would be closer to a voiceless consonant with a memory load than without. In other words, with a memory load, we'd predict that the size of the incomplete neutralisation stemming from the *incremental unitary planning effect* will decrease.

In contrast to 'incomplete neutralisation with a small effect size', 'incomplete neutralisation with a large effect size' appears to be rooted

---

[26] A reviewer suggests that the *incremental unitary planning effect* predicts an asymmetry in that if the triggering context is earlier than the target, there should be no incomplete neutralisation. The reviewer is definitely right that the proposed mechanism should not play a role when the triggering context occurs earlier and the target that undergoes neutralisation comes later, *if phonological processes are applied as soon as they are possible* – this on the face of it is reasonable to us, but needs independent justification. But, we agree with the reviewer that, minimally, the incomplete effect sizes will be smaller in such cases. We are currently not aware of any positive or negative examples of this prediction. Furthermore, other unidentified factors may still exert an influence and cause incomplete neutralisation – as long as we cannot assert 'all things being equal', there is no guarantee that two phonological units will be identical production. In fact, in our opinion, this is true for any theory of phonological representation that assumes that there are some non-linguistic effects on production, not just ours; that is, it is true for any theory that espouses the competence-performance distinction.

in phonological processes that are inherently optional. In other words, optionality is the triggering factor of incomplete neutralisation with a large effect size. We will use the term *simultaneous multiple planning effect* to refer to planning effect caused by optionality.

Incomplete neutralisation with a large effect size can be modelled under a formal perspective, wherein optional phonological processes are viewed as having multiple outputs simultaneously. The output of phonology in the case of an optional process would be a set of surface representations, instead of a unique surface representation (see Heinz 2020, for an identical claim); however, only one from the set of representations is selected and implemented in the production in any one instance.[27] When one of the representations is selected and implemented in the production, the other output is still part of the planning at each stage and will therefore exert a substantial influence on the planning and the subsequent implementation. As a result, the implemented surface representation is predicted to be closer to other possible surface representations in production; and this in turn results in incomplete neutralisation with a much larger effect size. Compare this case to that of the *incremental unitary planning effect*, wherein only one representation is a possible output from the phonology in any one instant of time during planning, and therefore the later outputs are expected to have a large influence due to recency. In the current case, both representations are outputted by the phonology as each instant of time (since the process is optional), and therefore, there is no specific recency bias for one over the other.

---

[27] A reviewer asks if such variation/optionality can be thought of as diglossia. To the reviewer's point, even if it is diglossia, there is still a need for multiple representations, but they would be stemming from different grammars ('languages'). Note, one could slightly modify our claim to include representations of a lexical item from multiple (very closely related) grammars instead of from a single grammar. We are in fact sympathetic to the view that the situation is diglossic in such cases; however, there needs to be empirical evidence in support of the view. Given that any language has multiple variable processes, the claim would then become one of multiglossia to account for all observed variation. One could of course argue using Ockham's razor that the multiglossic analysis of variation should be the natural starting point in the absence of evidence. However, it is not so simple here as the set of auxiliary assumptions are not identical in the multiglossic view and the multiple URs view; therefore, establishing simplicity is not straightforward. For example, the acquisition models would look quite different for the multiglossic view and our multiple URs view. Furthermore, at a theoretical level, such rampant multiglossia is simply a highly parameterised model, and it is difficult to know what sort of variation can't be accounted for by it beyond the fact that each dialect would be subject to the limits employed on any one grammar. In contrast, in our general view, a child balances the possibility of a new grammar against the possibility of proposing an optional process within the same grammar, and therefore tries to employ a simplicity metric (Chomsky and Halle 1965, 1968; Durvasula and Liter 2020). While the distinction is abstract, our view puts restrictions on what types of (co-)variation are possible. We refrain from discussing this issue further, as we feel we have entered the realm of idle speculation.

Let's take the Huai'an Tone 1 sandhi as an example: in Huai'an Tone 1 sandhi, underlying Tone 1 can surface as it is or undergoes Tone 1 sandhi to become Tone 3. When an underlying Tone 1 is mapped to an optional Tone 3 by the phonology, the other possible surface representation (Tone 1) still plays an important role in production, causing derived Tone 3 to deviate from underlying Tone 3 and become similar to underlying Tone 1. We'd like to clarify that we are not claiming that effect size is correlated with application rate per se. In fact, given our formalisation that the output of the phonology is a set of surface representations when there is optionality, there is no representation of the rate of optionality here at all. Our own results bear out this consequence that there is no connection between the rate of optionality and the actual effect size in the case where the effect size of incomplete neutralisation is large.

The data from Huai'an Tone 1 sandhi and Tone 4 sandhi that we presented in Du and Durvasula (2022) are shown in Figure 4 and Figure 5. In both figures, every data point represents a speaker. The x-axis represents the application rate of tone sandhi (number of token with tone sandhi applied/total number of token) and y-axis represents the effect size of incomplete neutralisation, which is the f0 difference between derived Tone 3 and underlying Tone 3 on raw pitch (f0 of derived Tone 3 – f0 of underlying Tone 3), relative to the average effect size. Non-parametric Spearman correlation analysis shows that there is no significant correlation for either Tone 1 sandhi ($\rho = 0.25$, p = 0.45) and Tone 4 sandhi ($\rho = 0.14$, p = 0.57). Note, following the analysis process in Du and Durvasula (2022), only derived Tone 3s that actually trigger another tone sandhi process are considered as real derived Tone 3s and analysed here.

Beyond our own results, the little available empirical evidence that we are aware of does seem to support that optionality results in neutralisation with a large effect size. Besides the two tone sandhi processes in Huai'an, another case

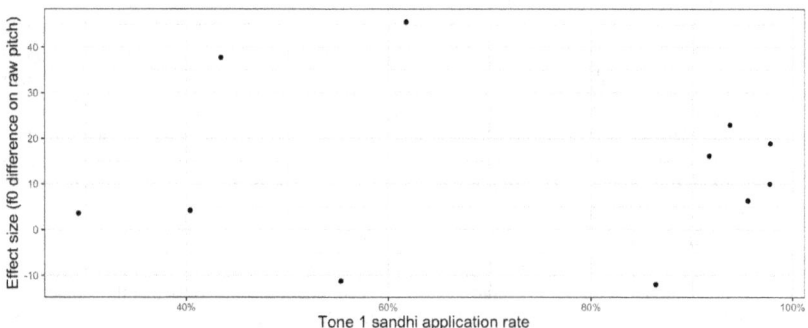

Figure 4 Relationship between Tone 1 application rate and effect size of incomplete neutralisation

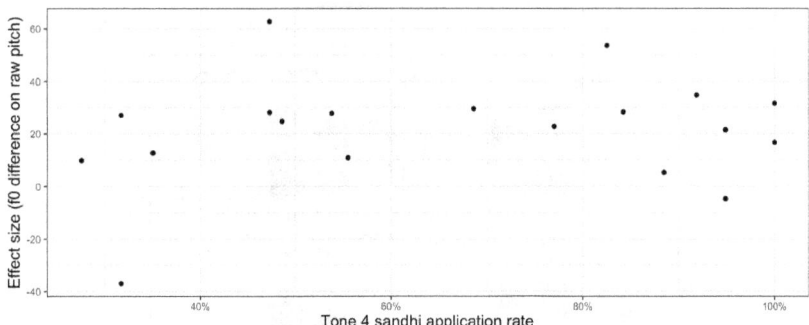

Figure 5 Relationship between Tone 4 application rate and effect size of incomplete neutralisation

is French schwa deletion (Beltzung and Wallet 2014; Fougeron and Steriade 1997; Lebel 1968; Rialland 1986). An example is shown in (9). Here, both [dəʁol] in (9a) and [dʁol] in (9b) can be the surface representations for the underlying representation /dəʁol/ 'role'. Although (9b–9c) are traditionally claimed to be phonologically identical, the segment [d] in (9b) where the schwa is deleted is not phonetically identical to its counterpart in (9c). Moreover, the effect size should be considered large by employing *Just Noticeable Difference* (Weber 1905) as the yardstick. The data are shown in Figure 6. The crucial comparisons are highlighted with the dotted line boxes.

9. Examples for French schwa deletion (Fougeron and Steriade 1997)

   (a)   de rôle   [dəʁol]   'role'
   (b)   d'rôle   [dʁol]   'role'
   (c)   drôle   [dʁol]   'funny'

In Fougeron and Steriade (1997) study, three measures were tested, namely the amount of linguopalatal contact, the duration of lingual occlusion, and the frequency of lenition. The consonant [d] in the deleted schwa case (/dəʁ/ → [dʁ]) is roughly equivalent to the case where the schwa is present (/dəʁ/ → [dəʁ]), and is quite far from the case with an underlying sequence (/dʁ/ → [dʁ]). It is worth pointing out that the values of all the measurements are not available in the original article, so we are unable to provide precise estimates. However, just by eyeballing, the duration difference of lingual occlusion gesture of the previous consonant [d] seems be around 10 ms. In a separate study by Beltzung and Wallet (2014), on the same process where the duration of consonant is the only measure, a similar durational difference of 9.98 ms was found in the following fricative. Although suggestions have been made that JND of consonant duration is usually at least 10 ms (Klatt 1976; Lehiste 1970;

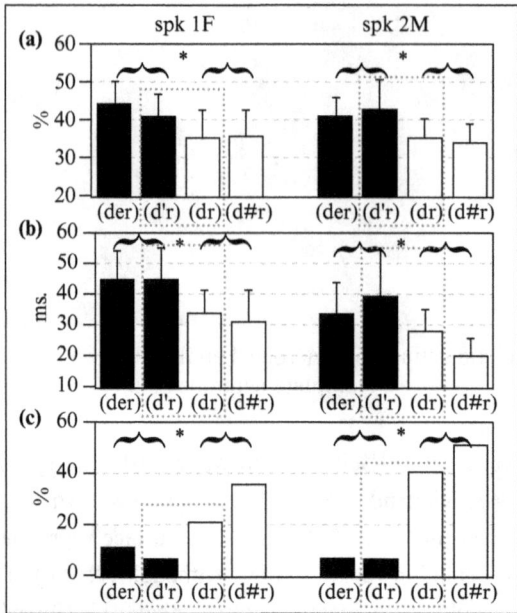

Figure 6 Comparison of phonetic cues among derived and underlying forms: (a) amount of linguopalatal contact in [d]; (b) duration of lingual occlusion gesture of [d]; (c) frequency of lenition of [d]. [Figure from Fougeron and Steriade (1997)]

Payne 2005), consensus has been reached in multiple subfields of psychology that JND should be defined in terms of proportion instead of raw numbers (Boring 1942; Hecht 1924; Vandenbussche et al. 1986). As shown in Figure 6, the differences are safe to be considered large for all three measures in terms of percentage. In Beltzung and Wallet's (2014) study, the fricative in the schwa deletion case (98.63 ms) is 11.26% longer than its underlying counterpart (88.66 ms), which can also be considered as large in terms of JND.

However, the findings in these two studies may not be totally convincing due to four separate issues. First, since the schwa deletion process is optional (Côté 2000), the possibility of incomplete neutralisation coming from an averaging effect cannot be eliminated.

Second, according to Côté (2000), the phonological process that occurs at the clitic boundary should be analysed as an insertion process instead of the deletion process assumed in previous studies discussed before (Beltzung and Wallet 2014; Fougeron and Steriade 1997). If such an analysis turns out to be valid, the found phonetic differences simply cannot lead to the conclusion of incomplete neutralisation.

Third, there is no independent evidence for phonological neutralisation. In fact, even if phonologically (9b) and (9c) may have the same segments, they may differ in terms of prosodic structure since (9b) contains both a clitic and a noun while (9c) is just a single noun. Therefore, the difference in phonetics may simply come from a prosodic structure difference, that is, there may be no phonological neutralisation at all, since there is no prosodic neutralisation.

Fourth, there are issues with the methodology, as relevant to question of effect sizes. For example, there were too few participants (only two speakers) in the experiment done by Fougeron and Steriade (1997), therefore assessing the effect size is difficult in such a case. Furthermore, in Beltzung and Wallet's (2014) study, the participants were explicitly instructed to read both the form where the schwa gets deleted and the form where the schwa does not undergo any phonological process and surface as it is – such a methodology leads to a high chance of generating unnatural speech.

Overall, more controlled future research and more careful justification for the putative phonological representations are needed in this particular French pattern to confirm that optionality leads to incomplete neutralisation with a large effect size.

A third and maybe more convincing case that supports the claim that optionality is a source of neutralisation with a large effect size is South Jeolla Korean. In this language, there is an optional phonological process whereby an underlying intermorphemic sequence /V_1h+pV_2/ can surface as [V_1p$^h V_2$] or as [V_1bV_2] (V = vowel) (Kang and Lee 2019; Lee et al. 2023). An example is given in (10). Lee et al. (2023) looked at the degree of glottal width during the post-stop vowel (V_2) by using an electroglottograph. They used the measures of Open Quotient and spectral tilt as proxies for glottal width. Figure 7 presents their results for the Open Quotient for the cases where the sequence /V_1h+pV_2/

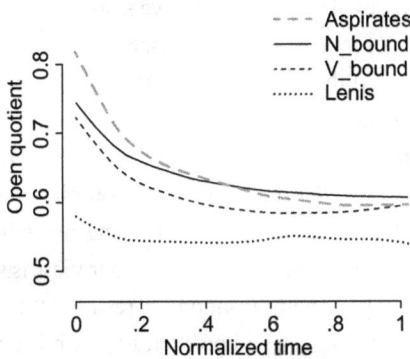

Figure 7 Comparison of Open quotient of vowels after underlying aspirated stop (Aspirates), derived voiced stop (N_bound and V_bound) and underlying voiced stops (Lenis) [Figure from Lee et al. (2023)]

putatively surface as [V₁bV₂]. As can be seen, there is substantial glottal opening in V₂ despite the sequence arguably surfacing as [V₁bV₂]. Furthermore, the crucial comparison between the lenis variant with the N_bound and V_bound variants, in the figure, suggests a substantial difference, particularly towards the beginning – the approximate difference of 0.15–0.2 is 1.5–2 times higher than the *Just Noticeable Difference* for Open Quotient (Henrich et al. 2003). While this is consistent with there being incomplete neutralisation with a large effect size, we'd like to point out that there is no independent evidence presented, based on phonological behaviour, for which surface alternant was observed for the measurement (the authors assume it to be [V₁bV₂] based on impressionistic coding). Consequently, the case needs to be studied further to see if there is independent evidence of the application of the process.

10. South Jeolla Korean non-coalescence process
    /pap+hana/ → [pabana] or [papʰana]

Returning to the main point in this section, we have proposed that there are ultimately (at least) two different types of incomplete neutralisation that don't stem from task effects/confounds: (a) incomplete neutralisation with a small effect size and (b) incomplete neutralisation with a large effect size. Our proposed explanations for both types of incomplete neutralisation in terms of different aspects of phonological planning satisfies all the desiderata listed in Section 2.3. Since they invoke no additional computations/representations; and only invoke otherwise necessary performance factors, the claims enjoy a simplicity of maintaining a relatively simple phonological framework that assumes discrete/abstract representation (8a). Next, since we offer separate explanations for incomplete neutralisation with a large effect size and incomplete neutralisation with a small effect size, the distribution of effect sizes among discovered cases can be naturally explained (8b); and we state clear criteria for where one would find each type of incomplete neutralisation, so if one were to find a contrary pattern, that would then be inconsistent with the theory (provided there are no confounding reasons, that is, provided the *all things being equal* clause applies). With regard to why 'over-neutralisation' is generally not observed in examined languages (8c), the theory views incomplete neutralisation as typically caused by the underlying category playing an indirect role in speech production in the examined cases. In this sense, our view is similar to those who have argued that incomplete neutralisation is a result of the blend of two distinct representations (see Section 2.4.2); however, for us, it is a blend of two different *surface representations*. Finally, since phonology is seen as consisting of discrete/abstract representations and mappings between such representations, it naturally accounts for the possibility of feeding interactions and explains why otherwise phonetically similar sounds might not participate in the change (8d–8e).

There are two further points we would like to make: first, our proposed explanations for incomplete neutralisation with a small effect size and incomplete neutralisation with a large effect size are compatible. For phonological processes that are inherently optional, both types of planning effects can exert influence in the direction of incomplete neutralisation at the same time because they are independent resources.

Second, in our proposed theoretical framework, 'over-neutralisation', can still appear in certain cases where there are *more than two* categories involved in the neutralisation process. Imagine a language that has a high tone category, a middle tone category, and a low tone category in the phonology, and there is a phonological process that maps an underlying high tone optionally to either a middle tone or a low tone in the surface. When the middle tone is picked up by the phonology, according to our theory, both the high tone and the low tone can still exert influence on the phonetics. Therefore, if the influence of low tone on speech production is stronger, the derived middle tone may not fall between the underlying high tone and the underlying middle tone to become a normal incomplete neutralisation, and an 'over-neutralisation' situation may occur when the derived middle tone falls between the underlying middle tone and the underlying low tone. Such a situation is of course rare in natural languages, which explains why 'over-neutralisation' is never observed so far. Future research is needed to verify the existence of 'over-neutralisation' in the specific contexts provided.

Given the paucity of cases with large effect sizes for incomplete neutralisation, there is need for further corroboration with further experimentation. Furthermore, our own previous experiments were not designed to test the claim of the optionality of a phonological process affecting the effect size of neutralisation, and introduced the different tone sandhi patterns in subtly different contexts and were between-subjects comparisons, which confounds the interpretation that the difference in the effect size for the different tone sandhi patterns is due to the optionality of some processes but not others. In Section 4, we will present a new experiment that controls for these confounds and show further support that the observed large effect size in incomplete neutralisation is related to optionality.

4 The Current Experiment

The current experiment has three purposes. First, it functions as a replication of the previous experiments on Huai'an high-register tone sandhis – we planned to confirm that Tone 1 and Tone 4 sandhis in Huai'an in fact have large effect sizes for phonetic incomplete neutralisation and that Tone 3 sandhi has a small effect size of phonetic incomplete neutralisation. Second, we run the experiment as a complete within-subject design, and thereby eliminate inter-subject variation as a possible source of the different effect sizes. Third, we argue that the presence of optionality is the triggering factor of incomplete neutralisation with a large effect size. In other words, only phonological processes that are inherently optional can have incomplete neutralisation with a large effect size. And again, we are not claiming that effect size is correlated with application rate per se, as clarified in Section 3.

4.1 Methods

4.1.1 Participants

We recruited eight native speakers of Huai'an Mandarin via personal relationships in Huai'an City. The age range was from forty-one to fifty-nine years old.[28] Among the speakers, four self-identified as female, and four as male. All the participants were born and raised in Huai'an City. These speakers had not participated in any linguistic studies before, nor had they heard about the concept of incomplete neutralisation prior to the experiment.

4.1.2 Stimuli

Following Du and Durvasula (2022), we tested three tone sandhi processes, namely Tone 1, Tone 4, and Tone 3, all of which apply postlexically and are completely productive. Crucially, we used postlexical processes to guard against the possibility that the incomplete neutralisation stems from memorised aspects of lexical entries. Furthermore, we used only right-branching utterances as in (6) because not enough left-branching utterances could be constructed by us given the paradigm (to be introduced immediately).

The stimuli were composed of trisyllabic sentences with each syllable forming a separate word, and they were divided into three groups. Each group was further divided into four sets as shown in (11–13). For the four sets testing Tone 1 sandhi, the third syllable was always Tone 1. The second syllable was one of the following possibilities: a) an underlying Tone 1 that optionally underwent Tone 1 sandhi to become Tone 3, b) an underlying Tone 3 that did not undergo any tone sandhi in this context. The first syllable was underlyingly a Tone 3 or a Tone 2. As a consequence of the possibilities in the second syllable, there were a few different possibilities for the first syllable, including: a)

---

[28] To minimise the influence of Standard Mandarin, we avoided younger speakers in this study.

an underlying Tone 3 that could undergo Tone 3 sandhi to become Tone 2 with reference to the second syllable, b) an underlying Tone 2 that did not undergo any tone sandhi in this context. The four sets were only different in tonal patterns but not in segmental content. The crucial comparison was between two tones in the second syllable. To be specific, the comparison was between the underlying Tone 3 in (11b) and the derived Tone 3 in (11d). This comparison allowed us to perfectly control for the surface context, while also establishing that the two tones are indeed categorical Tone 3s since they trigger Tone 3 sandhi on the preceding tone. Again, the set of possibilities also allowed us to look at an underlying Tone 1 in roughly the same surface context, as in the second possibility in (11c), for visual comparison. Finally, the crucial second syllable was always a voiceless unaspirated stop plus vowel sequence – voiceless unaspirated stops were chosen to make sure that there is a consistent way to annotate the acoustic onset of the vowel by referring to the burst of the stop.

The four sets testing Tone 4 sandhi were organised in the same fashion: the crucial comparison was between the underlying Tone 3 in (12b) and the derived Tone 3 in (12d). Again the crucial second syllable was always a voiceless unaspirated stop plus vowel sequence except one case where the syllable was a voiceless affricative plus vowel sequence.

For the Tone 3 sandhi process, since there are no tone sandhi processes in current Huai'an that can be triggered by Tone 2, it is impossible to establish derived Tone 2 from Tone 3 sandhi as categorical Tone 2. However, we will show that derived Tone 2 is phonetically highly similar to underlying Tone 2, which can provide at least some support that the annotation is appropriate. For the four sets testing Tone 3 sandhi, the third syllable is always Tone 3. The second syllable was one of the following possibilities: a) an underlying Tone 3 that optionally underwent Tone 3 sandhi with reference to the third syllable to become Tone 2, b) an underlying Tone 2 that did not undergo any tone sandhi in this context. The first syllable faced the same situation and was one of the following possibilities: a) an underlying Tone 3 that optionally underwent Tone 3 sandhi with reference to the third syllable to become Tone 2, b) an underlying Tone 2 that did not undergo any tone sandhi in this context. Since there is variation between Tone 2 and Tone 3 on the first syllable, a potential annotation mistake is more likely to occur in (13b) and (13d). To avoid this issue, the crucial comparison here is between the underlying Tone 2 of the second syllable in (13a) and the derived Tone 2 of the second syllable in (13c). This comparison allows us to perfectly control for the surface context. Finally, due to the scarcity of stimuli given the paradigm, we did not put a strict restriction on the onset of the crucial second syllable. We only made sure the rhyme was just one vowel.

11. Four sets of stimuli in the current experiment (Tone 1 sandhi) [the syllables crucial for the current comparison are underlined and boldface]
    (a) underlying T3 following underlying T2:
        /T2 T3 T1/ → [T2 T3 T1]
    (b) underlying T3 following underlying T3:
        /T3 T3 T1/ → [**T2 T3 T1**]
    (c) derived T3 following underlying T2:
        /T2 T1 T1/ → [T2 T3 T1] or [T2 T1 T1]
    (d) derived T3 following underlying T3:
        /T3 T1 T1/ → [**T2 T3 T1**] or [T3 T1 T1]

12. Four sets of stimuli in the current experiment (Tone 4 sandhi) [the syllables crucial for the current comparison are underlined and boldface]
    (a) underlying T3 following underlying T2:
        /T2 T3 T4/ → [T2 T3 T4]
    (b) underlying T3 following underlying T3:
        /T3 T3 T4/ → [**T2 T3 T4**]
    (c) derived T3 following underlying T2:
        /T2 T4 T4/ → [T2 T3 T4] or [T2 T4 T4]
    (d) derived T3 following underlying T3:
        /T3 T4 T4/ → [**T2 T3 T4**] or [T3 T4 T4]

13. Four sets of stimuli in the current experiment (Tone 3 sandhi) [the syllables crucial for the current comparison are underlined and boldface]
    (a) underlying T2 following underlying T2:
        /T2 T2 T3/ → [**T2 T2 T3**]
    (b) underlying T2 following underlying T3:
        /T3 T2 T3/ → [T3 T2 T3] or [T2 T2 T3][29]

---

[29] We have included this second possibility here as we have observed it in our fieldwork. There are two explanations that we think are reasonable to account for this pattern. First, the first syllable may be undergoing non-local Tone 3 sandhi to become Tone 2 with reference to the last syllable, which is also Tone 3. Note, this would be different from Standard Mandarin where low tone sandhi (Tone 3 sandhi) only applies on adjacent Tone 3 syllables (Chen 2000; Duanmu 2007). The second possible explanation is that there may be an undocumented tone sandhi pattern in Huai'an. Tone 3 may undergo tone sandhi to become Tone 2 with reference to the following Tone 2 syllable. Such a pattern is unlikely given that tone sandhis in Mandarin languages are usually dissimilation rules. However, if Tone 3 is represented as a low tonal target, and Tone 2 is represented as a low tonal target plus a high tonal target, then at the tonal target level, this new rule aligns with Obligatory Contour Principle (Leben 1973; McCarthy 1986; Yip 2002, amongst others). Since this set is irrelevant to the crucial comparison for Tone 3 sandhi, no

(c) derived T2 following underlying T2:
/T2 T3 T3/ → [**T2 T2 T3**]
(d) derived T2 following underlying T3:
/T3 T3 T3/ → [T3 T2 T3] or [T2 T2 T3]

The full stimuli list is summarised in Table 2, Table 3, and Table 4. Each participant produced a fully randomised list (that varied by participant) of four repetitions of all 72 test sentences at a natural speech rate, which meant each participant read a total of 288 sentences.

4.1.3 Procedure

The experiment was conducted entirely in Huai'an city. Each participant self-reported that they were born and raised in Huai'an and had not lived in other places for a long period of time in the past ten years. A trained research assistant did all the recordings using Audacity (Audacity Team 2022) and a Popu Line BK USB microphone on a Lenovo laptop. The recording process was conducted in quiet rooms that were either located in the participants' home or workplace. The real research question was not revealed to the participants, and instead they were told that the purpose of the study was to collect some general information on Huai'an. None of the participants reported noticing the minimal pairs or the real purpose of the study being on tones in the post-experimental interview.[30] The participants were instructed to read at a normal speech rate using their everyday voice. The participants were also encouraged to read through the stimulus list to be familiar with the reading materials before producing them.

4.1.4 Measurement

The recordings were manually annotated in Praat (Boersma and Weenink 2021), by the first author, who is a native speaker of Huai'an. An example is shown in Figure 8.

Both the first and second syllables were marked. The first syllable was marked to confirm that derived Tone 3 from Tone 1 sandhi and Tone 4 sandhi can in fact trigger Tone 3 sandhi on this syllable. An example is shown in Figure 8. The annotation file had five tiers in total. The first tier marked the

---

further discussions will be made except to point out that more work is needed on understading this sub-pattern.

[30] Note, this is important as it suggests that participants were not subject to the task effect of producing sentences/words to contrast them with others stimuli; a potential confound that we discussed in Section 2.

Table 2 Stimuli for the current experiment: Tone 1 sandhi

Characters	IPA	Pinyin	UR tones	SR tones
吴把车	u pa tɕi	wubache	231	231
吴鼓分	u ku fən	wugufen	231	231
吴把虾	u pa xa	wubaxia	231	231
吴摆虾	u pɛ xa	wubaixia	231	231
吴保车	u pɔ tɕi	wubaoche	231	231
吴保书	u pɔ su	wubaoshu	231	231
吴扒车	u pa tɕi	wubache	211	211/231
吴估分	u ku fən	wugufen	211	211/231
吴扒虾	u pa xa	wubaxia	211	211/231
吴掰虾	u pɛ xa	wubaixia	211	211/231
吴包车	u pɔ tɕi	wubaoche	211	211/231
吴包书	u pɔ su	wubaoshu	211	211/231
武把车	u pa tɕi	wobache	331	231
武鼓分	u ku fən	wogufen	331	231
武把虾	u pa xa	wobaxia	331	231
武摆虾	u pɛ xa	wobaixia	331	231
武保车	u pɔ tɕi	wobaoche	331	231
武保书	u pɔ su	wobaoshu	331	231
武扒车	u pa tɕi	wobache	311	311/231
武估分	u ku fən	wogufen	311	311/231
武扒虾	u pa xa	wobaxia	311	311/231
武掰虾	u pɛ xa	wobaixia	311	311/231
武包车	u pɔ tɕi	wobaoche	311	311/231
武包书	u pɔ su	wobaoshu	311	311/231

vowel of the syllable. The first zero crossing at the beginning of the voicing of the target vowel was identified as the onset, except if the vowel is preceded by an unaspirated stop; in the latter case, we made sure the onset of the vowel was marked after the burst of the unaspirated stop. The zero-crossing immediately following the vowel's final glottal pulse was identified as the offset. All other tiers marked the whole syllable to index phonological information and recording quality. The second tier indicated the position of the syllable inside the sentences where a first syllable was marked '1' and a second syllable was marked '2', the third tier contained the pinyin of the whole sentence followed by the underlying tone of the syllable. The fourth tier marked whether the syllable

Table 3 Stimuli for the current experiment: Tone 4 sandhi

Characters	IPA	Pinyin	UR tones	SR tones
吴保税	u pɔ suɛi	wubaoshui	234	234
吴躲肉	u to zɯ	wuduorou	234	234
吴把脉	u pa mɛ	wubamai	234	234
吴逮象	u tɛ ɕiã	wudaixiang	234	234
吴补炮	u pu pʰɔ	wubupao	234	234
吴举肉	u tɕu zɯ	wujurou	234	234
吴报税	u pɔ suɛi	wubaoshui	244	244/234
吴剁肉	u to zɯ	wuduorou	244	244/234
吴罢卖	u pa mɛ	wubamai	244	244/234
吴带象	u tɛ ɕiã	wudaixiang	244	244/234
吴布炮	u pu pʰɔ	wubupao	244	244/234
吴拒肉	u tɕu zɯ	wujurou	244	244/234
武保税	u pɔ suɛi	wubaoshui	334	234
武躲肉	u to zɯ	wuduorou	334	234
武把脉	u pa mɛ	wubamai	334	234
武逮象	u tɛ ɕiã	wudaixiang	334	234
武补炮	u pu pʰɔ	wubupao	334	234
武举肉	u tɕu zɯ	wujurou	334	234
武报税	u pɔ suɛi	wubaoshui	344	344/234
武剁肉	u to zɯ	wuduorou	344	344/234
武罢卖	u pa mɛ	wubamai	344	344/234
武带象	u tɛ ɕiã	wudaixiang	344	344/234
武布炮	u pu pʰɔ	wubupao	344	344/234
武拒肉	u tɕu zɯ	wujurou	344	344/234

underwent tone sandhi. And the last tier indicated the quality of the recording. Similar to our previous work on Huai'an (Du and Durvasula 2022), we only used productions of recordings that were marked 'good'. The f0 extraction, normalization, and visualization processes are identical to those in the previous experiment.

4.1.5 Results and Statistical Modelling

All data analyses in this Element were performed in R (R Core Team 2021) using the `tidyverse` suite of packages (Wickham et al. 2019). And the statistical modelling was done using the `lme4` package (Bates et al. 2021). The data

Table 4 Stimuli for the current experiment: Tone 3 sandhi

Characters	IPA	Pinyin	UR tones	SR tones
吴俘沈	u fu sən	wufushen	223	223
吴携果	u ɕi ko	wuxieguo	223	223
吴糊口	u xu kʰə	wuhukou	223	223
吴移沈	u i sən	wuyishen	223	223
吴扶许	u fu ɕy	wufuxu	223	223
吴埋果	u mɛ ko	wumaiguo	223	223
吴辅沈	u fu sən	wufushen	233	223
吴洗果	u ɕi ko	wuxieguo	233	223
吴唬狗	u xu kʰə	wuhukou	233	223
吴倚沈	u i sən	wuyishen	233	223
吴腐许	u fu ɕy	wufuxu	233	223
吴买果	u mɛ ko	wumaiguo	233	223
武俘沈	u fu sən	wufushen	323	323/223
武携果	u ɕi ko	wuxieguo	323	323/223
武糊口	u xu kʰə	wuhukou	323	323/223
武移沈	u i sən	wuyishen	323	323/223
武扶许	u fu ɕy	wufuxu	323	323/223
武埋果	u mɛ ko	wumaiguo	323	323/223
武辅沈	u fu sən	wufushen	333	323/223
武洗果	u ɕi ko	wuxieguo	333	323/223
武唬狗	u xu kʰə	wuhukou	333	323/223
武倚沈	u i sən	wuyishen	333	323/223
武腐许	u fu ɕy	wufuxu	333	323/223
武买果	u mɛ ko	wumaiguo	333	323/223

and analyses presented in this study are available at the following Open Science Foundation (OSF) repository: https://osf.io/wz62p.

The number of tokens for each possible combination of Underlying Representation (UR) and Surface Representation (SR) is summarised in Tables 5–7. The data used to calculate application rates are underlined and boldfaced. Thirty-six tokens were not marked as 'good' and excluded for the Tone 1 process, which accounts for 4.7% of all test stimuli for Tone 1 sandhi. Twenty-five tokens were not marked as 'good' and excluded for Tone 4 process, which accounts for 3.3% of all test stimuli for Tone 4 sandhi. Forty tokens were not marked as 'good' and excluded for Tone 3 process, which accounts for 5.2% of all test stimuli for Tone 3 sandhi.

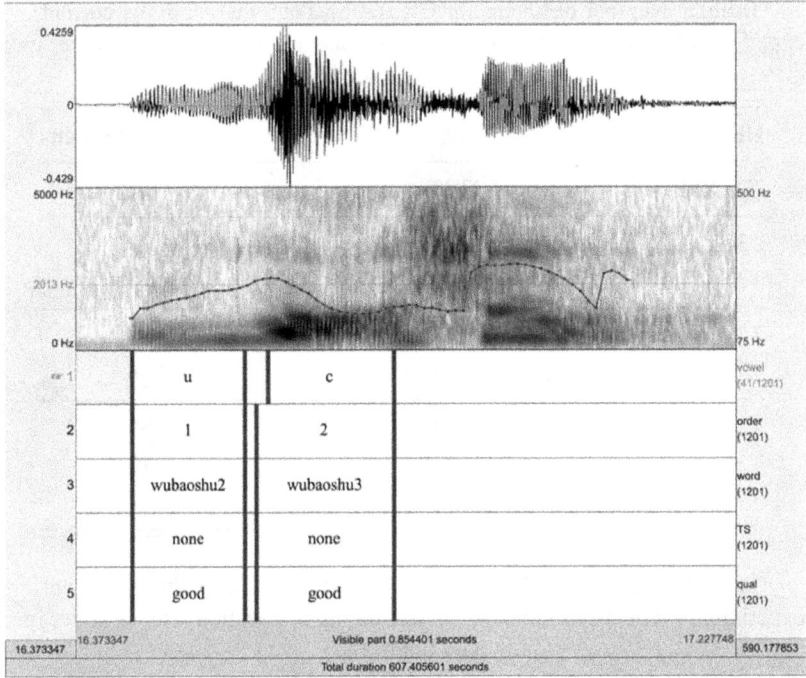

Figure 8 Annotation scheme of the current experiment (Tone 1)

The application rate of Tone 1 sandhi in the second syllable is 49.6%, the application rate of Tone 4 sandhi in the second syllable is 73.0%, and the application rate of Tone 3 sandhi in the second syllable is 96.5%. Therefore, it is safe to categorise Tone 1 and Tone 4 sandhi processes as optional and Tone 3 sandhi process as (close to) mandatory. We assume that the small rate of inapplication is not reflective of an optional process but result from performance errors.

The f0 values were z-score transformed by participant and by vowel to normalise the by-subject and by-vowel variation in pitch ranges. The z-score transformed f0 contours on the crucial second syllable are shown in Figures 9–11. Again for the Tone 1 and Tone 4 sandhi processes, the crucial comparison is between derived Tone 3 and underlying Tone 3; while for the Tone 3 sandhi process, the crucial comparison is between derived Tone 2 and underlying Tone 2. For Tone 1 and Tone 4 sandhi processes, as with our previous work (Du and Durvasula 2022), we also present the tone contour for an underlying Tone 1/Tone 4 in the same surface context for visual comparison. It is worth noting that here the tonal contours for crucial comparisons are also represented by lines that are based on the modelling results. We will present the statistical modelling strategy, which employs Growth Curve Analysis (Mirman 2017; Mirman et al. 2008), later in this subsection with the results.

Table 5 Number of tokens for UR and SR combination in the current experiment (Tone 1 sandhi; data for calculating application rates is underlined and boldfaced)

UR	SR	Number of tokens
T2T3T1	T2T3T1	188
T3T3T1	T3T3T1	7
T3T3T1	T2T3T1	180
T2T1T1	T2T1T1	**111**
T2T1T1	T2T3T1	**66**
T3T1T1	T3T1T1	**69**
T3T1T1	T3T3T1	**20**
T3T1T1	T2T3T1	**91**

Table 6 Number of tokens for UR and SR combination in the current experiment (Tone 4 sandhi; data for calculating application rates is underlined and boldfaced)

UR	SR	Number of tokens
T2T3T4	T2T3T4	185
T3T3T4	T3T3T4	14
T3T3T4	T2T3T4	166
T2T4T4	T2T4T4	**78**
T2T4T4	T2T3T4	**111**
T3T4T4	T3T4T4	**24**
T3T4T4	T3T3T4	**113**
T3T4T4	T2T3T4	**52**

Based on the visual inspection of the data, the existence of incomplete neutralisation is clear for Tone 1 and Tone 4 sandhi, wherein the derived Tone 3 is quite distinct from the underlying Tone 3. In contrast, for Tone 3 sandhi process, the derived Tone 2 and underlying Tone 2 are highly similar with regard to tonal contour, although there is a small but observable difference between them. The visual inspection seems to bear out the observations in Du and Durvasula (2022), but with a within-subjects comparison and with stimuli that don't have the confound of structural differences. Each stimuli is right-branching and made of three syllables. The first syllable is always the subject, the second

Table 7 Number of tokens for UR and SR combination in the current experiment (Tone 3 sandhi; data for calculating application rates underlined and boldfaced)

UR	SR	Number of tokens
T2T2T3	T2T2T3	178
T3T2T3	T3T2T3	86
T3T2T3	T2T2T3	90
T2T3T3	T2T3T3	<u>9</u>
T2T3T3	T2T2T3	<u>**179**</u>
T3T3T3	T3T3T3	<u>**0**</u>
T3T3T3	T2T3T3	<u>**4**</u>
T3T3T3	T3T2T3	<u>**39**</u>
T3T3T3	T2T2T3	<u>**143**</u>

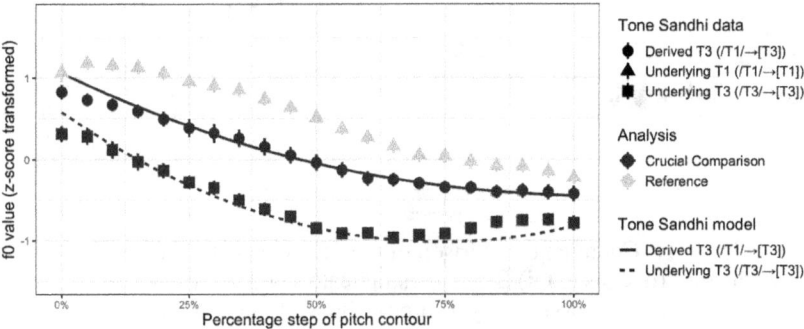

Figure 9 Contours comparison of the second syllable in the current experiment (Tone 1 sandhi) (Error bars indicate standard error; lines represent Growth Curve Analysis model fits with the best model)

syllable is always the verb, and the third syllable is always the object. We will show that incomplete neutralisation exists for all three tone sandhi processes using statistical modelling.

It is also worth noting that the contour shape of the derived Tone 3 from Tone 1 in the current experiment is different from that in Du and Durvasula (2022). As a reminder, in that experiment, the contour shape of derived Tone 3 from Tone 1 starts as an underlying Tone 3 and ends as an underlying Tone 1, as shown in Figure 2. However, in the current experiment, the starting point of derived Tone 3 from Tone 1 is between underlying Tone 3 and underlying Tone 1, and the end-point seems to be close to that of underlying Tone 1 but there is still clear gap between them. The contour shape of derived Tone 3 from

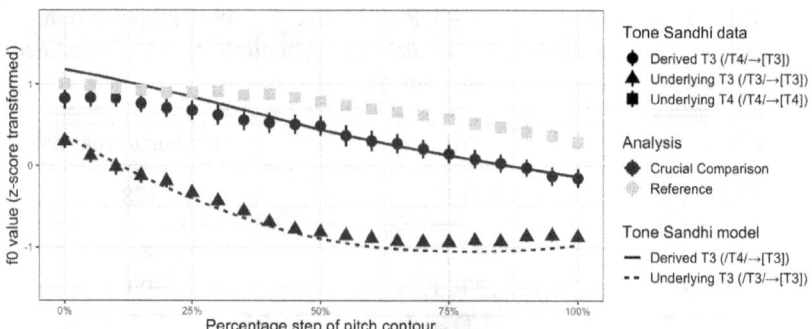

Figure 10 Contours comparison of the second syllable in the current experiment (Tone 4 sandhi) (Error bars indicate standard error; lines represent Growth Curve Analysis model fits with the best model)

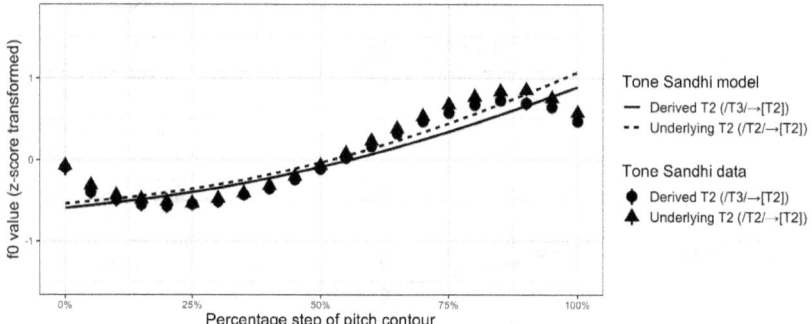

Figure 11 Contours comparison of the second syllable in the current experiment (Tone 3 sandhi) (Error bars indicate standard error; lines represent Growth Curve Analysis model fits with the best model)

Tone 4 in the current experiment is consistent with what was observed before (Figure 3).

For the purposes of statistical modelling, to answer the crucial question of whether or not the underlying and derived tones have incompletely neutralised, we used just the two-group factor (underlying Tone 3 versus derived Tone 3 for Tone 1 and Tone 4 sandhi, underlying Tone 2 versus derived Tone 2 for Tone 3 sandhi). The results turn out to support the observation that the neutralisation is indeed incomplete phonetically.

In dealing with time-course data, traditional techniques like t-tests and ANOVA have to divide continuous time into multiple time bins and therefore have to make multiple comparisons. This method has been argued by Mirman (2017) to be problematic for increasing the risk of false positives. Since each time bin incurs the nominal 5 per cent false positive rate implied by alpha <0.05, the overall false positive rate with multiple time bins and multiple comparisons will be much higher than a single comparison.

To solve this issue, many different analysis methods have then been developed including Smooth Spline Analysis of Variance (SS-ANOVA) (Wang 1998), Generalized Additive Models (GAM) (Hastie and Tibshirani 1995) and Growth Curve Analysis (GCA) (Mirman 2017; Mirman et al. 2008). In this Element, we follow Chen et al. (2017) and model f0 contours using Growth Curve Analysis.[31]

Growth Curve Analysis uses multilevel linear regression to avoid multiple comparisons and has been argued to be a useful modelling technique in different fields (Baldwin and Hoffmann 2002; McArdle and Nesselroade 2003, amongst others). To apply Growth Curve Analysis in Huai'an tones, we started with a simple model as in (14) (Mirman et al. 2008).

14. Growth Curve Analysis basic model

$$Y^{ij} = (\gamma^{00} + \zeta^{0i}) + (\gamma^{10} + \zeta^{1i}) \times Time^{ij} + \epsilon^{ij}$$

Here i is the ith f0 (z-score transformed) contour and j is the jth time point, and Y^{ij} is the f0 (z-score transformed) value for i^{th} contour at j^{th} time point. γ^{00} is the population average value for the intercept, ζ^{0i} is individual variation on the intercept, γ^{10} is the population average value for the fixed effect of time, ζ^{1i} is individual variation on the fixed effect of time and ϵ^{ij} is the error term. To optimise the model for the data, we employed higher-order polynomial functions, and allowed individuals to vary on each term only when those terms reached significance according to chi-square likelihood ratio tests (Chen and Li 2021; Chen et al. 2017, amongst others).[32]

As noted in Du and Durvasula (2022), one needs relevant theoretical/prespecified restrictions in modelling phonetic data, including f0 contours. A Tone Bearing Unit (TBU), which is assumed to be the syllable or the rhyme or the nucleus of the rhyme, has been widely argued to be associated with at most three tonal targets in Mandarin phonology (Bao 1990, 1992; Duanmu 1994, amongst others). As a result, the most complex tones have one change

---

[31] We have re-analysed the results in terms of Barks using the method described in Traunmüller (1990) and did not see any change in the pattern of results. The relevant code and the corresponding plots are part of the OSF repository: https://osf.io/wz62p.

[32] The procedure recommended by Chen and Li (2021) and Chen et al. (2017) is a forward selection process that is potentially anti-conservative (Barr et al. 2013), and may result in a higher number of significant results. However, our results in the current study are largely in line with our previous experimental results both in direction and in effect size (despite being different in that the current results involve within-subject comparisons). This suggests that our results are not false positives.

of direction in f0 contours and will appear as U-shaped contours. Examples include a high-low-high tone or low-high-low tone. To conform to the general agreement in Mandarin tonal phonology, we only considered up to second-order functions to ensure that the final model is not more complex than a U-shape contour. Also, orthogonal polynomials were used to make sure that the linear and quadratic terms were not correlated (Mirman 2017). After optimising the model by including all significant terms, we first treated underlying Tone and derived Tone as the same and modelled them as one single contour to get Model 1. Then we built models that treated them as different, namely, models that included a tone sandhi condition (underlying Tone versus derived Tone) to do model comparison. Based on Model 1, the tone sandhi condition is first allowed to affect only the intercept to get Model 2. Then the tone sandhi condition is allowed to affect both the intercept and the linear term to get Model 3. Finally, the tone sandhi condition is allowed to affect all the fixed effects, including the intercept, the linear term, and the quadratic term, and the outcome is Model 4. A Chi-square likelihood ratio test was used to determine whether two minimally different models differ significantly.

For the Tone 1 sandhi process, the addition of a tone sandhi condition improved the model on the intercept as shown by comparing Model 1 and Model 2 ($x^2(1) = 455.19, p < 0.01$), the linear term as shown by comparing Model 2 and Model 3 ($x^2(1) = 6.77, p < 0.01$), and the quadratic term as shown by comparing Model 3 and Model 4 ($x^2(1) = 7.51, p < 0.01$). Figure 9 shows how the best model (Model 4) with the assumption of tone sandhi affecting every fixed effect fits the observed data. And the parameter estimates for the full model are summarised in Table 8.

For the Tone 4 sandhi process, the addition of a tone sandhi condition improved the model on the intercept as shown by comparing Model 1 and Model 2 ($x^2(1) = 929.04, p < 0.01$), not on the linear term as shown by comparing Model 2 and Model 3 ($x^2(1) = 0.31, p = 0.58$), and on the quadratic term as shown by comparing Model 3 and Model 4 ($x^2(1) = 17.22, p < 0.01$). Figure 10 shows how the best model (Model 4) with the assumption of tone sandhi affecting the intercept and the quadratic term fits the observed data. And the parameter estimates for the full model are summarised in Table 9.

As with the other two tone sandhi processes, for the Tone 3 sandhi process, the addition of a tone sandhi condition improved the model on the intercept as shown by comparing Model 1 and Model 2 ($x^2(1) = 14.09, p < 0.01$), but not on the linear term as shown by comparing Model 2 and Model 3 ($x^2(1) = 1.53, p = 0.22$), or on the quadratic term as shown by comparing Model 3 and Model 4 ($x^2(1) = 0.66, p = 0.42$). Figure 11 shows how the best model (Model 2) with the assumption of tone

Table 8 Parameter estimates of the full model (Model 4) for Tone 1 sandhi process with the assumption of tone sandhi affecting every fixed effect (baseline: derived Tone 3)

	Estimate	Std. Error	t	p
Intercept	0.10	0.02	4.78	<0.01
Linear	−17.60	1.52	−11.55	<0.01
Quadratic	5.01	1.27	3.95	<0.01
Tone Sandhi: Intercept	−0.67	0.03	−23.04	<0.01
Tone Sandhi: Linear	0.47	1.18	0.40	0.69
Tone Sandhi: Quadratic	4.45	1.18	3.78	<0.01

Table 9 Parameter estimates of the full model (Model 4) for Tone 4 sandhi process with the assumption of tone sandhi affecting every fixed effect (baseline: derived Tone 3)

	Estimate	Std. Error	t	p
Intercept	0.50	0.10	5.09	<0.01
Linear	−16.98	1.39	−12.26	<0.01
Quadratic	2.20	1.44	1.52	0.15
Tone Sandhi: Intercept	−1.18	0.03	−35.92	<0.01
Tone Sandhi: Linear	0.71	1.23	0.56	0.58
Tone Sandhi: Quadratic	5.29	1.27	4.18	<0.01

sandhi affecting only the intercept fits the observed data. And the parameter estimates for the full model are summarised in Table 10.

With regard to effect size, as predicted by our theory laid out in Section 3, the effect sizes of incomplete neutralisation are large for the two optional phonological processes (Tone 1 and Tone 4 sandhis), while the effect size of incomplete neutralisation for the mandatory phonological process (Tone 3) is very small.

The raw f0 differences (f0 of derived Tone 3 − f0 of underlying Tone 3 for Tone 1 sandhi; f0 of derived Tone 3 − f0 of underlying Tone 3 for Tone 4 sandhi; f0 of derived Tone 2 − f0 of underlying Tone 2 for Tone 3 sandhi) of each step for Tone 1, Tone 4, and Tone 3 sandhis are summarised in Table 11, Table 12, and Table 13. We first calculated the mean difference for individual speakers at each step. Then for each step, we took an average among the eight speakers to calculate the raw f0 difference.

For Tone 1 sandhi, the mean difference in f0 between underlying Tone 3 and derived Tone 3 across all steps is 19 Hz, which is about three times the *Just*

Table 10 Parameter estimates of the full model (Model 4) for Tone 3 sandhi process with the assumption of tone sandhi affecting every fixed effect (baseline: derived Tone 2)

	Estimate	Std. Error	t	p
Intercept	<0.01	0.03	0.03	0.98
Linear	19.92	2.79	7.14	<0.01
Quadratic	3.50	1.96	1.79	0.11
Tone Sandhi: Intercept	0.08	0.02	3.76	<0.01
Tone Sandhi: Linear	1.18	0.95	1.24	0.22
Tone Sandhi: Quadratic	0.78	0.95	0.82	0.42

Table 11 f0 Difference (derived Tone 3 – underlying Tone 3) of each step in the current experiment (Tone 1 sandhi)

Step	f0 difference (Hz)	Step	f0 difference (Hz)
0	14	11	24
1	10	12	23
2	13	13	22
3	16	14	20
4	19	15	21
5	19	16	20
6	20	17	19
7	22	18	17
8	22	19	16
9	22	20	18
10	24		

Noticeable Difference of f0 value (7 Hz) for Mandarin speakers (Jongman et al. 2017). Moreover, across from step 8 to step 12 of Tone 1 sandhi, the f0 difference is over 22 Hz, which is more than three times the *Just Noticeable Difference*. Similarly, for Tone 4 sandhi, the mean difference in f0 between underlying Tone 3 and derived Tone 3 across all steps is 41 Hz, which is more than five times the *Just Noticeable Difference* of f0 value (7 Hz) for Mandarin speakers. And across from step 2 to step 20 of Tone 4 sandhi, the f0 difference is over 35 Hz, which is more than five times the *Just Noticeable Difference*. Therefore, based on our criterion, we are able to clearly define the Tone 1 and Tone 4 sandhi processes as incomplete neutralisation with large effect sizes.

Table 12 f0 difference (derived Tone 3 – underlying Tone 3) of each step in the current experiment (Tone 4 sandhi)

Step	f0 difference (Hz)	Step	f0 difference (Hz)
0	22	11	46
1	34	12	46
2	38	13	46
3	36	14	46
4	37	15	44
5	39	16	42
6	40	17	42
7	42	18	38
8	46	19	39
9	49	20	40
10	47		

Table 13 f0 difference (derived Tone 2 – underlying Tone 2) of each step in the current experiment (Tone 3 sandhi)

Step	f0 difference (Hz)	Step	f0 difference (Hz)
0	0	11	0
1	−1	12	0
2	−1	13	0
3	0	14	0
4	0	15	−1
5	0	16	−2
6	0	17	−2
7	0	18	−4
8	1	19	−4
9	1	20	−5
10	2		

In contrast, for Tone 3 sandhi, the mean difference in f0 between underlying Tone 2 and derived Tone 2 across all steps is only 1 Hz. Moreover, across all steps of Tone 3 sandhi, the f0 difference is less than the *Just Noticeable Difference*. Therefore, based on our criterion, we are able to clearly define the Tone 3 sandhi process as incomplete neutralisation with a small effect size.

To summarise the results of the new experiment, optional phonological processes (Tone 1 and Tone 4 sandhis) have large effect sizes in incomplete neutralisation, while for the mandatory phonological process (Tone 3), the effect size is rather small. Again, by comparing Tone 1, Tone 4, and Tone 3 sandhis of Huai'an using exactly the same experimental paradigm on the same group of speakers, previously identified interacting factors, including speaker group variation, prosodic structure (boundary strength), and speech rate, are better controlled for.

We'd like to note that there is a potential problem with the analysis. Since the tone sandhi conditions were impressionistically coded by the first author, it is reasonable to suspect the accuracy. It is worth remembering that, for the parts where the crucial comparison is between derived Tone 3 from Tone 1 and Tone 4 sandhi processes and underlying Tone 3, we took into consideration only derived Tone 3 that actually triggers Tone 3 sandhi in the first syllable. However, if the coding is not accurate on the application of Tone 3 sandhi in the first syllable (so, whether or not it is a derived Tone 2), syllables that have not undergone Tone 1 sandhi or Tone 4 sandhi may be mistaken for derived Tone 3s. It would have been optimal if we could show through independent phonological behaviour that Tone 3 sandhi has actually been triggered. If derived Tone 2 from Tone 3 sandhi has the same phonological behaviour as underlying Tone 2, we can be sure that Tone 3 sandhi has actually been triggered in the first syllable. However, there are no phonological processes that can be triggered by Tone 2 in Huai'an. Although Tone 2 sandhi (Tone 2 + Tone 2 → Tone 3 + Tone 2) has been observed in Huai'an (Wang and Kang 2012), the tone sandhi process was not observed in our fieldwork in early 2020 probably due to the influence of the standard language, as is generally observed in other languages (Labov 1963; Milroy 2001, amongst others). Furthermore, no other phonological processes have been identified that can be triggered by Tone 2 in Huai'an. Overall, the analytic technique of depending on phonological behaviour does not work for derived Tone 2 in Huai'an and we are forced to rely only on phonetic evidence for the Tone 2 identity of the derived rising tone. We will show that, derived Tone 2s in the first syllable derived by Tone 3 sandhi, which itself is triggered by a derived Tone 3 in the second syllable from Tone 1 or Tone 4 sandhis are indeed phonetically highly similar with underlying Tone 2s.

For the part of the analysis testing Tone 1 and Tone 4 sandhi processes, the tone contours for the relevant first syllables are shown in Figure 12 and Figure 13. We also present the tone contours for underlying Tone 3s in the first syllable that come from derived Tone 3s failing to trigger Tone 3 sandhi on the preceding syllables. By doing so, a three-way visual comparison is possible at the position of the first syllable under the same phonological environment, that is, before derived Tone 3 (from either Tone 1 or Tone 4). As we have done in presenting the data for the crucial second syllables, here the tonal

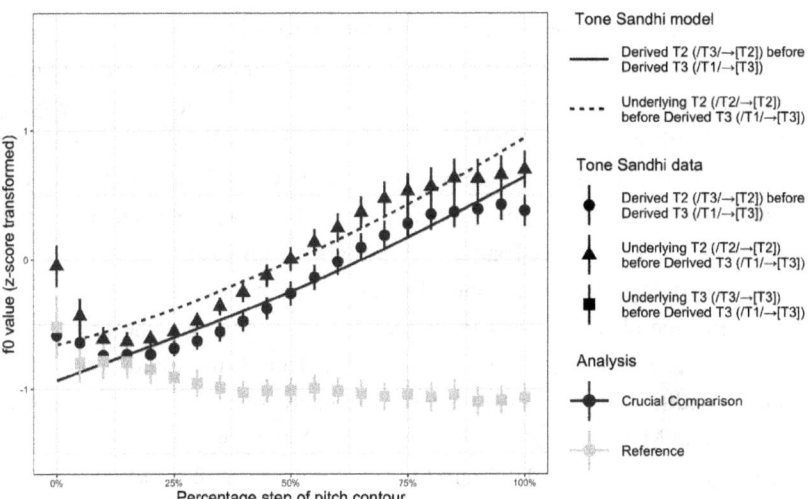

Figure 12 Contours comparison of the first syllable in the current experiment (Tone 1 sandhi) (Error bars indicate standard error; lines represent Growth Curve Analysis model fits with the best model)

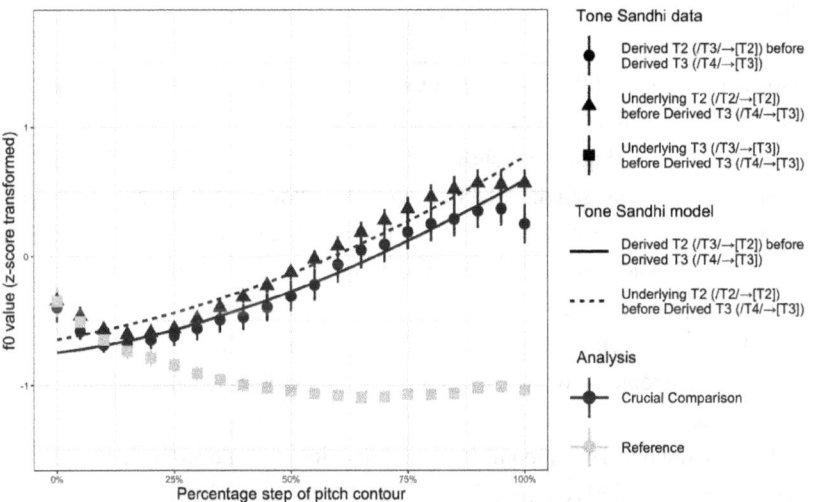

Figure 13 Contours comparison of the first syllable in the current experiment (Tone 4 sandhi) (Error bars indicate standard error; lines represent Growth Curve Analysis model fits with the best model)

contours for the crucial comparison (underlying Tone 2 versus derived Tone 2) are also represented by lines representing model fits. We will present the results of statistical modelling later in this subsection.

Based on the visual inspection of the data, the derived Tone 2s that are the results of Tone 3 sandhi triggered by following derived Tone 3s are phonetically highly similar to the corresponding underlying Tone 2s with regard to the f0 contour. The f0 contours of the derived Tone 2 and underlying Tone 2 in both figures are phonetically very different from those of corresponding underlying Tone 3s. Furthermore, as with the other tone sandhi processes discussed in this Element, there is incomplete phonetic neutralisation in both cases of the derived Tone 2 and the underlying Tone 2 in the first syllable. Gaps between the derived Tone 2 and the underlying Tone 2 in both cases are obvious.

The modelling method remained the same for contour tones, and the results do support the observation of incomplete neutralisation. For the case of the derived Tone 2 before the derived Tone 3 from Tone 1, the addition of a Tone Sandhi condition improved the model on the intercept as shown by comparing Model 1 and Model 2 ($x^2(1) = 66.41, p < 0.01$), but not on the linear term as shown by comparing Model 2 and Model 3 ($x^2(1) = 3.20, p = 0.07$), or the quadratic term as shown by comparing Model 3 and Model 4 ($x^2(1) < 0.01, p = 0.95$).

For the case of the derived Tone 2 before the derived Tone 3 from Tone 4, the addition of a Tone Sandhi condition also only improved the model on the intercept as shown by comparing Model 1 and Model 2 ($x^2(1) = 20.59, p < 0.01$), but not on the linear term as shown by comparing Model 2 and Model 3 ($x^2(1) = 0.09, p = 0.76$), or the quadratic term as shown by comparing Model 3 and Model 4 ($x^2(1) = 0.10, p = 0.75$).

Figure 12 and Figure 13 show how the best models (Model 2) with the assumption of tone sandhi affecting only the intercept fit the observed data. And the parameter estimates for the full models are summarised in Table 14 and Table 15. The f0 difference (f0 of underlying Tone 2 – f0 of derived Tone 2) of each step is summarised in Table 16 and Table 17. As mentioned, we first calculated the mean difference for individual speakers at each step. Then for each step, we took an average among the eight speakers to calculate the raw f0 difference.

Despite the observed incomplete neutralisation, the substantial phonetic difference between derived Tone 2 and underlying Tone 3 in both cases and the phonetic similarity between derived Tone 2 and underlying Tone 2 in both cases are difficult to account for by any mechanism known to us other than Tone 3 sandhi – it cannot simply be random variation or a co-articulatory change. Therefore, the impressionistic coding was in our opinion appropriate for the new experiment.

There is one issue that our experiment cannot resolve – Is it the case that the very nature of the phonetics involved with the different tones (and tone sandhis) result in the degree of incomplete neutralisation? For example, Tone 3 has mostly a low f0 (in non-final contexts), while the other two tones have higher f0

Table 14 Parameter estimates of the full model (Model 4) with the assumption of tone sandhi affecting every fixed effect (data: first syllable in the current experiment (Tone 1 sandhi); baseline: derived Tone 2)

	Estimate	Std. Error	t	p
Intercept	−0.21	0.07	−3.02	0.02
Linear	15.40	3.34	4.60	<0.01
Quadratic	2.09	1.66	1.25	0.24
Tone Sandhi: Intercept	0.24	0.03	8.26	0.13
Tone Sandhi: Linear	1.93	1.08	1.79	0.07
Tone Sandhi: Quadratic	0.06	1.07	0.06	0.95

Table 15 Parameter estimates of the full model (Model 4) with the assumption of tone sandhi affecting every fixed effect (data: first syllable in the current experiment (Tone 4 sandhi); baseline: derived Tone 2)

	Estimate	Std. Error	t	p
Intercept	−0.19	0.09	−2.13	0.06
Linear	15.69	1.93	8.11	<0.01
Quadratic	2.25	1.23	1.82	0.09
Tone Sandhi: Intercept	0.13	0.03	4.56	<0.01
Tone Sandhi: Linear	0.31	1.05	0.29	0.77
Tone Sandhi: Quadratic	0.33	1.04	0.32	0.75

ranges. It is logically possible that this phonetic fact drives the degree of incompleteness. We are unable to exclude this possibility based on our data. However, we are conducting further experiments on related languages with different sets of optional processes to see if it bears out, and our preliminary observations suggest this explanation is unlikely.

5 Conclusion

In this Element, we presented a detailed discussion of the foundational claims of *classic generative phonology*, wherein phonological knowledge is just one of the inputs to the phonetics, or performance more generally. We showed that the view has often been misunderstood and misdescribed in the literature. This has led to a common misunderstanding of generative phonology, which we call the *common strawman view of discrete representations* view. This latter view was already thought to be incorrect within the classic generative paradigm and, therefore, modern arguments against the latter view don't automatically extend

Table 16 f0 Difference (underlying Tone 2 – derived Tone 2) of each step for first syllable in the current experiment (Tone 1 sandhi)

Step	f0 difference (Hz)	Step	f0 difference (Hz)
0	5	11	10
1	8	12	10
2	5	13	10
3	5	14	11
4	5	15	11
5	6	16	11
6	7	17	11
7	8	18	11
8	9	19	11
9	10	20	10
10	10		

Table 17 f0 Difference (underlying Tone 2 – derived Tone 2) of each step for first syllable in the current experiment (Tone 4 sandhi)

Step	f0 difference (Hz)	Step	f0 difference (Hz)
0	14	11	2
1	4	12	1
2	1	13	1
3	−2	14	0
4	−1	15	0
5	−1	16	0
6	1	17	0
7	2	18	−1
8	3	19	0
9	3	20	2
10	3		

to the former. Furthermore, we showed that much of the problematic evidence presented in the literature either doesn't bear on the central abstract representational claims of *classic generative phonology*, or is actually consistent with it once we take into account equivalent auxiliary hypotheses. As we noted in Du and Durvasula (2022), 'there is no tension between incomplete phonetic neutralisation and categorical phonological neutralisation for the *classic generative phonology*; instead, the actual mystery as per this view has always been with any observed cases of complete phonetic neutralisation stemming from a process of phonological neutralisation'. In fact, the space of phonetic measurements is an infinite dimension space, so we are not even sure how one goes about establishing complete phonetic neutralisation. Potentially, one possibility is to show that there is no observable difference in the 'important cues'; but note, that argument then is different from claiming complete phonetic neutralisation.

We hope to have convincingly shown that the extant evidence is indeed consistent with at least one theory of abstract/discrete representations, namely the *classic generative phonology* view. However, we also pointed out that consistency with a theory is a rather weak result if the space of possibilities is very large. Notably, this issue of consistency being a weak criterion is if anything a worse problem for theories that incorporate high-dimensional and gradient representations. Furthermore, it is problematic if we claim consistency with vague claims, as there is no real way to assess inconsistency in such cases. Therefore, we need to develop clear and specific *explanations*, not just accounts, if we are to make progress. For this reason, we explored a particular instantiation of the debate outlined within research on the phenomenon of incomplete neutralisation, and showed the same arguments play out in this corner of phonetic research in exactly the same way.

In order to make progress on the issue, we suggested five desiderata (also presented in Du (2023) and Du and Durvasula (2022)) that we believe any theory of incomplete neutralisation should achieve in order to *explain* and not just account for the phenomenon:

15. Desiderata for a theory of incomplete neutralisation
    (a) The simplest account of why incomplete neutralisation exists as a phenomenon.
    (b) An *explanation* for the actual distribution of effect sizes among different phonological processes.
    (c) An *explanation* of why 'over-neutralisation' is never observed.
    (d) An *explanation* of how a feeding interaction is possible with another process if there is phonetically incomplete neutralisation.
    (e) Related to 15d, an *explanation* of why incompletely neutralised segments can trigger the process, but other phonetically similar segments do not.

Consistent with these desiderata, we proposed two specific but related hypotheses about how to account for incomplete neutralisation of different effect sizes in terms of planning effects, along lines that we consider necessary for independent reasons. For 'incomplete neutralisation with a small effect size', we proposed an *incremental unitary planning effect*, wherein two (or more precisely, multiple) separate and antagonistic surface representations are planned for the same underlying representations at different points of the planning, and the more recently planned surface representations have a stronger influence on the outcome. As a consequence, the actual utterance is going to have incomplete neutralisation with a small effect size. For 'incomplete neutralisation with a large effect size', we proposed a *simultaneous multiple planning effect* that applies in the case of optional processes. As per this, since the process is optional, the phonology outputs a set of possible surface representations (where one of them is identical to the underlying representation when the process doesn't apply) out of which one of them is chosen to be the actual production. Even in this case, there are two (possibly multiple if there are many possible outputs of the process) antagonistic surface representations; however, neither is more recent than the other. Therefore, no matter which one is ultimately chosen for production, the other planned surface representation will have a substantial effect. As a consequence, the actual utterance is going to have incomplete neutralisation with a large effect size. Importantly, this latter phenomenon, as we present it, is not expected to be sensitive to the actual application rate of the optional process, but to the presence of optionality itself.

We'd like to note that, as with any auxiliary hypothesis, the ones we present in this Element could very well be wrong, but importantly that still doesn't entail the claim that the larger framework is wrong (as is true for any scientific framework (Lakatos 1968)). However, we believe being precise and making clear/testable predictions is an important step to learning about the underlying system; therefore, there's much to learn from being wrong.

In line with these predictions, we presented the results of a production study focussed on tone sandhi patterns in Huai'an Mandarin that have feeding interactions – a crucial aspect of the patterns that inform us that indeed the process is phonological. The experiment confirmed our predictions that a mandatory tone sandhi pattern (Tone 3 sandhi) resulted in a very small effect size of incomplete neutralisation, while two other optional tone sandhi patterns (Tone 1 and Tone 4 sandhi) resulted in much larger effect sizes of incomplete neutralisation. Crucially, none of these incomplete neutralisation effects could simply be from memorised lexical entries as we specifically used post-lexical processes to guard against this possibility.

A further aspect of the results that we would like to highlight is the fact that the derived Tone 3 from Tone 1 sandhi in the current experiment had a different shape from that in Du and Durvasula (2022), while the derived Tone 3 from Tone 4 sandhi had a similar shape to that in Du and Durvasula (2022).

This also adds to our claim, and that of *classic generative phonology*, that subtle aspects of the experiment design, and sometimes simple random variation in the results can account for what might be otherwise thought to be meaningful differences in phonetic manifestations. Consequently, not every aspect of the phonetic output is relevant in learning about the underlying phonological knowledge. In short, phonetic results (as with any data) should not be taken at face value, but should be assessed in the context of a well-specified and justifiable set of competing hypotheses/theories.

We would like to end the Element with two additional notes: First, while throughout this Element we have primarily focussed on incomplete neutralisation in the spatial domain, our proposed auxiliary hypotheses also have an influence on the temporal domain. For example, the second author is part of an ongoing study on incomplete neutralisation between underlying palatalised consonants (/p^j/ → [p^j]) and derived palatalised consonants (/pj/ → [p^{j}j]) in Russian (Oh et al. 2023). They observed that, though both types of consonants are indeed phonetically palatalised, the palatal gesture was more delayed with respect to the lip gesture in the case of the derived palatalised consonant. This is what the *incremental unitary planning effect* would predict. In the case of the derived palatalised consonant, earlier planning events will not involve a palatalised consonant, as the relevant consonant is not palatalised in the underlying representation, but only later planning events would involve a palatalised consonant. Consequently, one expects there to be a delay in the phonetic manifestation of the palatalisation on the consonant. This is exactly what was observed by Oh et al. (2023). Note further that, given our hypothesis, there is no way for the derived palatalised consonant to have an earlier palatalisation gesture than an underlying palatalised segment; consequently, we believe the hypothesis truly explains the observed pattern, and doesn't just account for it.

Second and finally, though we have primarily focussed on production and how it interfaces with phonological knowledge in this Element, the issues we raise also apply to the available perceptual and neurolinguistic data arguing for high-dimensional gradient representations. There have been multiple observations of speaker-specificity in perception. Such results have been used to argue that there is no real speaker normalisation, and that lexical items are clouds of high-dimensional gradient (exemplar) representations (see Goldinger 1996, 1998; Johnson 1997; Pierrehumbert 2016, for discussion). In fact, such claims have sometimes been adjoined by additional claims that the theory of an independent speech normalisation process is unfalsfiable (Goldinger 1998). However, we do not see why this should be the case. First, observations of speaker-specificity in perception don't automatically form an argument against abstract/discrete phonological representation. At best, they show information beyond phonological knowledge is used in perception – a claim that is perfectly consistent with the *classic generative phonology* view as we discussed in this Element. In theory, such results can be accounted for by positing (thoughtful and speaker-specific) speech normalisation models. And there is clear evidence of early and consistent speech normalisation resulting in much more abstract/discrete representations (Chang et al. 2010; Oganian et al. 2023; Sjerps et al. 2019). Furthermore, in very recent work, Xie et al. (2023) argue that when computationally precise models of speaker-specificity in perception are implemented, the extant evidence is inconclusive between '(1) low-level, pre-linguistic, signal normalization, (2) changes in/selection of linguistic representations, or (3) changes in post-perceptual decision-making' (p. 377). The first and third possibilities would mesh perfectly with *classic generative phonology*, while the third possibility of changing/expanding the representations is possible for both discrete/abstract and high-dimensional gradient representations. Furthermore, as with production, the same issue of the space of possibilities being uncountably infinite hounds the high-dimensional gradient representations in perception. Consequently, we ourselves are far more sanguine about the prospects of abstract/discrete phonological representations and independent speaker-specific models (and other models of socilinguistically relevant dimensions) in dealing with evidence that has been provided in favour of speaker-specific exemplar representations.

References

Allen, W. Sidney (1953). Phonetics in ancient India. Oxford: Oxford University Press.

Archangeli, Diana (1988). 'Aspects of underspecificationtheory'. Phonology 5.2, pp. 183–207. https://doi.org.10.1017/S0952675700002268.

Audacity Team (15 May 2022). Audacity. Version 2.3.2. www.audacityteam.org/.

Baddeley, Alan (2000). 'The episodic buffer: A new component of working memory?'. Trends in cognitive sciences 4.11, pp. 417–423.

Baldwin, Scott A. and John P. Hoffmann (2002). 'The dynamics of self-esteem: A growth-curve analysis'. Journal of youth and adolescence 31.2, pp. 101–113.

Bao, Zhiming (1990). 'Fanqie languages and reduplication'. Linguistic inquiry 21.3, pp. 317–350. http://www.jstor.org/stable/4178680.

Bao, Zhiming (1992). 'Toward a typology of tone sandhi'. In Annual Meeting of the Berkeley Linguistics Society. Ed. by Laura A. Buszard-Welcher, Jonathan Evans, David Peterson, Lionel Wee and William Weigel. Vol. 18. 2, pp. 1–12.

Barr, D. J., R. Levy, C. Scheepers, and H. J. Tily (2013). 'Random effects structure for confirmatory hypothesis testing: Keep it maximal'. Journal of memory and language Ed. by Dale J. Barr, Roger Levy, Christoph Scheepers, and Harry J. Tily. 68.3, pp. 1–26. https://doi.org.10.1016/j.jml.2012.11.001.

Bates, Douglas, Martin Mächler, Ben Bolker, and Steven Walker (2021). Lme4: Linear mixed-effects models using 'Eigen' and S4. https://CRAN.R-project.org/package=lme4.

Beltzung, Jean-Marc and Lucille Wallet (2014). 'Réajustements temporels et syllabiques après l'effacement optionnel du schwa en français'. In SHS Web of Conferences. Ed. by Franck Neveu, Peter Blumenthal, Linda Hriba, Annette Gerstenberg, Judith Meinschaefer, and Sophie Prévost. Vol. 8. EDP Sciences, pp. 1227–1236.

Benua, Laura (1995). 'Identity effects in morphological truncation'. In University of Massachusetts Occasional Papers, 18, Ed. by Jill N. Beckman, Laura W. Dickey, and Suzanne Urbanczyk. GLSA, UMass Amherst, pp. 33–66.

Berko, Jean (1958). 'The child's learning of English morphology'. WORD 14.2–3, pp. 150–177. https://doi.org.10.1080/00437956.1958.11659661.

Boersma, Paul and David Weenink (2021). Praat. Version 6.1.41. www.praat.org/.

Boring, Edwin Garrigues (1942). 'Sensation and perception in the history of experimental psychology'. New York: Appleton-Century-Crofts.

Braver, Aaron (2014). 'Imperceptible incomplete neutralization: Production, non-identifiability, and non-discriminability in American English flapping'. Lingua 152, pp. 24–44.

Braver, Aaron (2019). 'Modelling incomplete neutralisation with weighted phonetic constraints'. Phonology 36.1, pp. 1–36.

Braver, Aaron and Shigeto Kawahara (2016). 'Incomplete neutralization in Japanese monomoraic lengthening'. In Proceedings of the Annual Meetings on Phonology. Vol. 2. Ed. by Adam Albright and Michelle A. Fullwood.

Bromberger, Sylvain and Morris Halle (2000). 'The ontology of phonology (revised)'. Phonological knowledge: Conceptual and empirical issues. Ed. by Noel Burton-Roberts, Philip Carr, and Gerard Docherty, pp. 19–37.

Browman, Catherine P. and Louis H. Goldstein (1988). 'Some notes on syllable structure in articulatory phonology'. Phonetica 45, pp. 140–155. https://doi.org.10.1159/000261823.

Browman, Catherine P. and Louis H. Goldstein (1989). 'Articulatory gestures as phonological units'. Phonology 6.2, pp. 201–251. https://doi.org.10.1017/S0952675700001019.

Browman, Catherine P. and Louis H. Goldstein (1990). 'Tiers in articulatory phonology, with some implications for casual speech'. In Papers in Laboratory Phonology. Vol. 1. Ed. by John Kingston and Mary E. Beckman. Cambridge: Cambridge University Press, pp. 341–376. https://doi.org.10.1017/CBO9780511627736.019.

Brown, Roger and David McNeill (1966). 'The "tip of the tongue" phenomenon'. Journal of verbal learning and verbal behavior 5.4, pp. 325–337.

Burzio, Luigi (1994). Principles of English stress. Cambridge: Cambridge University Press.

Burzio, Luigi (1998). 'Multiple correspondence'. Lingua 104.12, pp. 79–109.

Bybee, Joan L. (1994). 'A view of phonology from a cognitive and functional perspective'. Cognitive linguistics 5.4, pp. 285–305.

Bybee, Joan L. (2001). 'Phonology and language use'. Cambridge: Cambridge University Press.

Chang, Edward F., Jochem W. Rieger, Keith Johnson, Mitchel S. Berger, Nicholas M. Barbara, and Robert T. Knight (2010). 'Categorical speech representation in human superior temporal gyrus'. Nature neuroscience 13.11, pp. 1428–1432.

Chao, Yuen-Ren (1930). 'A system of tone letters'. Le maître phonétique 30, pp. 24–27.

References

Chen, Matthew Y. (2000). Tone sandhi: Patterns across Chinese dialects. Cambridge: Cambridge University Press.

Chen, Si and Bin Li (2021). 'Statistical modeling of application completeness of two tone sandhi rules'. Journal of chinese linguistics 49.1, pp. 106–141.

Chen, Si, Caicai Zhang, Adam G McCollum, and Ratree Wayland (2017). 'Statistical modelling of phonetic and phonologised perturbation effects in tonal and non-tonal languages'. Speech communication 88, pp. 17–38.

Cheng, Chin-Chuan (2011). A synchronic phonology of Mandarin Chinese. Vol. 4. The Hague: Mouton.

Chomsky, Noam (1959). Language 35.1, pp. 26–58. www.jstor.org/stable/411334.

Chomsky, Noam (1964). 'Current issues in linguistic theory'. In the Hague: Mouton. In The Structure of Language. Ed. by Janet A. Fodor and J. J. Katz, pp. 85–112.

Chomsky, Noam (1965). Aspects of the theory of syntax. Cambridge, MA: MIT Press.

Chomsky, Noam (1983). 'Some conceptual shifts in the study of language'. In Many Questions? Essays in Honor of Sidney Morgenbesser. Ed. by Leigh S. Cauman, Issac Levi, Charles D. Parsons, and Robert Schwartz, Indianapolis, IN: Hackett pp. 154–169. Indianapolis, IN: Hackett.

Chomsky, Noam (1955/1975). The logical structure of linguistic theory. New York: Plenum Press.

Chomsky, Noam and Morris Halle (1965). 'Some controversial questions in phonological theory'. Journal of linguistics 1.2, pp. 97–138.

Chomsky, Noam and Morris Halle (1968). The sound pattern of English. New York: Harper and Row.

Chomsky, Noam and Andrea Moro (2022). The secrets of words. Cambridge, MA: MIT Press.

Chomsky, Noam, Ian Roberts, and Jeffrey W atumull (2023). 'Noam Chomsky: The false promise of chatgpt'. The New York Times 8.

Clements, George N. (1985). 'The geometry of phonological features'. Phonology yearbook 2, pp. 225–252.

Côté, Marie-Hélène (2000). 'Consonant cluster phonotactics: A perceptual approach'. PhD diss. Cambridge, MA, USA: Massachusetts Institute of Technology.

Cowan, Nelson (2008). 'What are the differences between long-term, short-term, and working memory?' Progress in brain research 169, pp. 323–338.

Coward, Harold G. and K. Kunjunni Raja (2015). The Encyclopedia of Indian Philosophies, Volume 5: The Philosophy Vol. 1235. Princeton: Princeton University Press.

Cummins, Robert (2000). '"How does it work?" vs. "What are the laws?" Two conceptions of psychological explanation'. Ed. by F. Keil and R. Wilson, pp. 117–145.

Dell, Gary S., Kristopher D. Reed, David R. Adams, and Antje S. Meyer (2000). 'Speech errors, phonotactic constraints, and implicit learning: A study of the role of experience in language production'. Journal of experimental psychology: Learning memory and cognition 26.6 pp. 1355–1367. www.scopus.com/inward/record.uri?eid=2-s2.0-0034328780&doi=10.1037%2f0278-7393.26.6.1355&partnerID=40&md5=c8cb6bc14994624319205747ae408f5b.

Dinnsen, Daniel A. and Jan Charles-Luce (1984). 'Phonological neutralization, phonetic implementation and individual differences'. Journal of phonetics 12.1, pp. 49–60.

Dmitrieva, Olga (2005). 'Incomplete neutralization in Russian final devoicing: Acoustic evidence from native speakers and second language learners'. PhD diss. University of Kansas.

Dresher, B. Elan (2009). The contrastive hierarchy in phonology. Cambridge Studies in Linguistics. Cambridge: Cambridge University Press. https://doi.org.10.1017/CBO9780511642005.

Du, Naiyan (2023). 'Against strict correspondence between phonetic measurements and phonological representations'. PhD diss. Michigan State University.

Du, Naiyan and Karthik Durvasula (2022). 'Phonetically incomplete neutralization can be phonologically complete: Evidence from Huai'an Mandarin'. Phonology 39.4, pp. 559–595.

Duanmu, San (1994). 'Against contour tone units'. Linguistic inquiry 25.4, pp. 555–608.

Duanmu, San (2007). The phonology of standard chinese. Oxford: Oxford University Press.

Duhem, Pierre Maurice Marie (1954). The aim and structure of physical theory. Princeton: Princeton University Press.

Durvasula, Karthik and Adam Liter (2020). 'There is a simplicity bias when generalising from ambiguous data'. Phonology 37.2, pp. 177–213.

Ernestus, Mirjam and R. Harald Baayen (2006). 'The functionality of incomplete neutralization in Dutch: The case of past-tense formation'. Laboratory phonology 8.1, pp. 27–49.

Ferreira, Fernanda and Benjamin Swets (2002). 'How incremental is language production? Evidence from the production of utterances requiring the computation of arithmetic sums'. Journal of memory and language 46.1, pp. 57–84.

Firth, John Rupert Firth (1948). 'Sounds and Peosodies'. Transactions of the philological society 47.1, pp. 127–152. https://doi.org/10.1111/j.1467-968X.1948.tb00556.x.

Flemming, Edward (1995). 'Auditory features in phonology'. PhD diss. University of California, Los Angeles.

Flemming, Edward (2001). 'Scalar and categorical phenomena in a unified model of phonetics and phonology'. Phonology 18.1, pp. 7–44.

Fougeron, Cécile and Donca Steriade (1997). 'Does deletion of French schwa lead to neutralization of lexical distinctions?' In Eurospeech. Vol. 2, pp. 943–946.

Fourakis, M. and Gregory K. Iverson (1984). 'On the "Incomplete Neutralization" of German Final Obstruents'. Phonetica 41, pp. 140–149. https://doi.org.10.1159/000261720.

Gafos, Adamantios I. and Stefan Benus (2006). 'Dynamics of phonological cognition'. Cognitive science 30.5, pp. 905–943.

Gerfen, Chip (2002). 'Andalusian codas'. Probus, 14.2, pp. 247–277.

Glanzer, Murray and Anita R. Cunitz (1966). 'Two storage mechanisms in free recall'. Journal of verbal learning and verbal behavior 5.4, pp. 351–360.

Goldinger, Stephen D. (1996). 'Words and voices: Episodic traces in spoken word identification and recognition memory'. Journal of experimental psychology: Learning memory and cognition 22.5, pp. 1166–1183. https://doi.org.10.1037/0278-7393.22.5.1166.

Goldinger, Stephen D. (1997). 'Words and voices: Perception and production in an episodic lexicon'. Talker variability in speech processing. Ed. by Keith Johnson and John W. Mullennix. San Diego: Academic Press, pp. 33–66.

Goldinger, Stephen D. (1998). 'Echoes of echoes? An episodic theory of lexical access'. Psychological review 105.2, pp. 251–279. https://doi.org.10.1037/0033-295X.105.2.251.

Goldrick, Matthew and Sheila E. Blumstein (2006). 'Cascading activation from phonological planning to articulatory processes: Evidence from tongue twisters'. Language and cognitive processes 21.6, pp. 649–683. https://doi.org.10.1080/01690960500181332.

Goldrick, Matthew and Jennifer Cole (2023). 'Advancement of phonetics in the 21st century: Exemplar models of speech production'. Journal of phonetics 99, p. 101254. https://doi.org/10.1016/j.wocn.2023.101254.

Gouskova, Maria and Nancy Hall (2009). 'Acoustics of unstressable vowels in Lebanese Arabic'. In Phonological argumentation: Essays on evidence and motivation. Ed. by Steve Parker. London: Equinox, pp. 203–225.

Greene, Anthony J., Colin Prepscius, and William B. Levy (2000). 'Primacy versus recency in a quantitative model: Activity is the critical distinction'. Learning and memory 7.1, pp. 48–57.

Hale, Mark, Madelyn Kissock, and Charles Reiss (2007). 'Microvariation, variation, and the features of universal grammar'. Lingua 117.4, pp. 645–665.

Halle, Morris (1954). Why and how do we study sounds of speech? Ed. by Hugo J. Mueller. Verlag nicht ermittelbar.

Halle, Morris (1959a). 'Questions of linguistics'. Il nuovo cimento (1955–1965) 13.2, pp. 494–517.

Halle, Morris (1959b). The sound pattern of Russian: A linguistic and acoustical investigation. The Hague: Mouton.

Halle, Morris (1962). 'Phonology in generative grammar'. Word 18.1, pp. 54–72.

Halle, Morris (1978). 'Comment on S. Singh's rejoinder to the review of his distinctive features: Theory and validation [J. Acoust. Soc. Am. 62, 276–277 (1978)]'. The journal of the acoustical society of America 63.1, pp. 278–279. https://pubs.aip.org/asa/jasa/article-pdf/63/1/278/11461012/278_1_online.pdf.

Halle, Morris. (1985). Speculation about the representation of words in memory. In Victoria Fromkin (Ed.), *Phonetic linguistics*, pp. 101–114. New York: Academic Press.

Hammarberg, Robert (1976). 'The metaphysics of coarticulation'. Journal of phonetics 4.4, pp. 353–363.

Hammarberg, Robert (1982). 'On redefining coarticulation'. Journal of phonetics 10.2, pp. 123–137.

Hastie, Trevor and Robert Tibshirani (1995). 'Generalized additive models for medical research'. Statistical methods in medical research 4.3, pp. 187–196.

Hay, Jennifer, Stefanie Jannedy, and Norma Mendoza-Denton (1999). 'Oprah and/ay: Lexical frequency, referee design and style'. In Proceedings of the 14th International Congress of Phonetic Sciences. University of California Berkeley, CA, pp. 1389–1392.

Hecht, Selig (1924). 'The visual discrimination of intensity and the Weber-Fechner law'. The journal of general physiology 7.2, p. 235.

Heinz, Jeffrey (2020). 'Deterministic analysis of optional processes'. Language Sciences Colloquium Series, University of California, Irvine.

Henrich, Nathalie, Gunilla Sundin, Daniel Ambroise, Christophe d'Alessandro, Michele Castellengo, and Boris Doval (2003). 'Just noticeable differences of open quotient and asymmetry coefficient in singing voice'. Journal of voice 17.4, pp. 481–494.

Huang, Borong and Xudong Liao (2017). Xiandai hanyu [Contemporary Chinese]. Higher Education Press.
Ito, Junko and Armin Mester (2003). 'On the sources of opacity in OT: Coda processes in German'. In The Syllable in Optimality Theory. Ed. by Caroline Féry and Ruben van de Vijver. Cambridge University Press, pp. 271–303. https://doi.org.10.1017/CB09780511497926.012.
Itô, Junko (1990). 'Prosodic Minimality in Japanese'. In CLS 26-II: Papers from the Parasession on the Syllable in Phonetics and Phonology. Ed. by Michael Ziolkowski, Manuela Noske, and Karen Deaton, 213–239.
Itô, Junko and Armin Mester (1999). 'The phonological lexicon'. In Natsuko Tsujimura (ed.) The handbook of Japanese linguistics. Malden, Mass. & Oxford: Blackwell, pp. 62–100.
Japan Broadcasting Corporation (1998). The Japanese language pronunciation and accent dictionary. Tokyo: NHK.
Jiao, L. (2004). 'Huai'an fangyan de shengdiao fenxi [The analysis of tones in Huai' an dialect]'. Master's diss. Tianjin, China: Tianjin Normal University.
Johnson, Keith (1997). 'Speech perception without speaker normalisation'. In Talker variability in speech processing. Ed. by Keith Johnson and John W. Mullennix. San Diego: Academic Press, pp. 145–165.
Johnson, Keith and John W. Mullennix, eds. (1997). Talker variability in speech processing. San Diego: Academic Press.
Jongman, Allard, Zhen Qin, Jie Zhang, and Joan A. Sereno (2017). 'Just noticeable differences for pitch direction, height, and slope for Mandarin and English listeners'. The journal of the acoustical society of America 142.2, EL163–EL169. https://doi.org.10.1121/1.4995526.
Kahn, Daniel (1976). 'Syllable-based generalizations in English phonology'. Phd diss. MIT. https://dspace.mit.edu/handle/1721.1Z16397.
Kang, Hijo and Hyo-Young Lee (2019). 'The realizations of /h/ in Seoul and Gwangju Koreans'. The linguistic society of Korea 84, pp. 175–198.
Keating, Patricia A. (1985). 'Universal phonetics and the organization of grammars'. Phonetic linguistics: Essays in honor of Peter Ladefoged. Ed. by Victoria A. Fromkin. New York: Academic Press, pp. 115–132.
Keating, Patricia A. (1990). 'The window model of coarticulation: Articulatory evidence'. In Papers in Laboratory Phonology. Ed. by John Kingston and Mary E. Beckman. Vol. 1. Cambridge University Press, pp. 451–470. https://doi.org.10.1017/CB09780511627736.026.
Kenstowicz, Michael J. (1994). Phonology in generative grammar. Oxford: Blackwell.
Kenstowicz, Michael J. (1995). 'Morpheme invariance and uniform exponence'. Ms. MIT and Rutgers Optimality Archive.

Kenstowicz, Michael J. and Charles Kisseberth (1977). Topics in phonological theory. New York: Academic Press.

Kharlamov, Viktor (2012). 'Incomplete neutralization and task effects in experimentally-elicited speech: Evidence from the production and perception of word-final devoicing in Russian'. PhD diss. University of Ottawa.

Kilbourn-Ceron, Oriana and Matt Goldrick (2021). 'Variable pronunciations reveal dynamic intra-speaker variation in speech planning'. Psychonomic bulletin and research. https://doi.org.10.3758/s13423-021-01886-0.

Kiparsky, Paul (1968). 'How abstract is phonology?' In Three dimensions of linguistic theory. Ed. by Osama Fujimura. Tokyo: Taikusha, pp. 5–56.

Kiparsky, Paul (1978). 'Analogical change as a problem for linguistic theory'. Studies in the linguistic sciences 8.2, pp. 77–96.

Klatt, Dennis H. (1976). 'Linguistic uses of segmental duration in English: Acoustic and perceptual evidence'. The journal of the acoustical society of America 59.5, pp. 1208–1221.

Kruszewski, Mikołaj (1883/1995). 'Očrk Nauki O Jazyke (An outline of linguistic science). Writings in general linguistics'. Ed. by K. Koerner, pp. 43–173.

Kuo, Yu-ching, Yi Xu, and Moira Yip (2007). 'The phonetics and phonology of apparent cases of iterative tonal change in Standard Chinese'. In Experimental studies in word and sentence prosody. Ed. by Carlos Gussenhoven and Tomas Riad. Berlin: Mouton de Gruyter, pp. 211–237.

Labov, William (1963). 'The social motivation of a sound change'. Word 19.3, pp. 273–309.

Lakatos, Imre (1968). 'Changes in the problem of inductive logic'. In Studies in Logic and the Foundations of Mathematics. Vol. 51. Elsevier, pp. 315–417.

Lakatos, Imre (1970). 'Falsification and the methodology of scientific research programmes'. Criticism and the Growth of Knowledge: Proceedings of the International Colloquium in the Philosophy of Science, London, 1965. Ed. by Imre Lakatos and Alan Musgrave. Vol. 4. Cambridge University Press, pp. 91–196. https://doi.org.10.1017/CBO9781139171434.009.

Lebel, Jean-Guy (1968). 'Allongement compensatoire de quelques consonnes par suite de la chute du'. Revue de phonétique appliquée 7, pp. 53–77.

Leben, William Ronald (1973). 'Suprasegmental phonology'. PhD diss. Cambridge, MA: Massachusetts Institute of Technology.

Lee, Seunghun J., Julian Villegas, and Mira Oh (2023). 'The Non-coalescence of /h/ and incomplete neutralization in South Jeolla Korean'. Language and speech 66.2, pp. 442–473.

Lehiste, Ilse (1970). Suprasegmentals. Cambridge, MA: MIT Press.

Lionnet, Florian (2017). 'A theory of subfeatural representations: The case of rounding harmony in Laal'. Phonology 34.3, pp. 523–564.

Lowe, John J. (2020). 'Segmental phonology in Ancient India?' Language 96.2, e97–e113.

Lowe, John J. (2024). Modern linguistics in ancient India. Cambridge: Cambridge University Press.

Lyons, J. (1974). 'Linguistics'. Encyclopaedia Britannica 10, p. 1002.

Manaster Ramer, Alexis (1996). 'A letter from an incompletely neutral phonologist'. Journal of phonetics 24.4, pp. 477–489.

Mascaró, Joan (1987). 'Underlying voicing recoverability of finally devoiced obstruents in Catalan'. Journal of phonetics 15.2, pp. 183–186.

Matsui, Mayuki (2015). 'Roshiago ni okeru yuuseisei no tairitsu to tairitsu no jakka: Onkyo to chikaku. [Voicing contrast and contrast reduction in Russian: Acoustics and perception]'. PhD diss. Hiroshima University.

McArdle, John J. and John R. Nesselroade (2003). 'Growth curve analysis in contemporary psychological research'. Handbook of psychology, pp. 447–480.

McCarthy, John J. (1986). 'OCP effects: Gemination and antigemination'. Linguistic inquiry 17.2, pp. 207–263.

McCollum, Adam G. (2019). 'Gradient morphophonology: Evidence from Uyghur vowel harmony*'. Proceedings of the Annual Meeting on Phonology (AMP) 2018, San Diego, CA, USA.

McCollum, Adam G., K. Durvasula, and X. Abudushalamu (2023). 'Is harmony in Uyghur really gradient?' Annual Meeting on Phonology 2023.

Mei, Tsu—lin (1977). 'Tones and tone sandhi in 16th century Mandarin'. Journal of Chinese linguistics, pp. 237–260.

Milner, Brenda (1970). 'Memory and the medial temporal regions of the brain'. Biology of memory 23, pp. 31–59.

Milroy, James (2001). 'Language ideologies and the consequences of standardization'. Journal of sociolinguistics 5.4, pp. 530–555.

Mirman, Daniel (2017). Growth curve analysis and visualization using R. CRC press.

Mirman, Daniel, James A. Dixon, and James S. Magnuson (2008). 'Statistical and computational models of the visual world paradigm: Growth curves and individual differences'. Journal of memory and language 59.4, pp. 475–494.

Mohanan, Karuvannur Puthanveettil (1986). The theory of lexical phonology. Vol. 6. Dordrecht, Holland: D. Reidel Publishing Company.

Mori, Yoko (2002). 'Lengthening of Japanese monomoraic nouns'. Journal of phonetics 30.4, pp. 689–708.

Moro, Andrea (2016). Impossible languages. MIT press.

Myers, James and Jane Tsay (2008). 'Neutralization in Taiwan Southern Min tone sandhi'. Interfaces in Chinese phonology: Festschrift in honor of Matthew Y. Chen on his 70th Birthday, pp. 47–78.

Nelson, Scott and Jeffrey Heinz (2021). Incomplete neutralization and the blueprint model of production. Ed. by Katherine Hout, Anna Mai, Adam McCollum, Sharon Rose, and Matthew Zaslansky.

Nicenboim, Bruno, Timo B. Roettger, and Shravan Vasishth (2018). 'Using metaanalysis for evidence synthesis: The case of incomplete neutralization in German'. Journal of phonetics 70, pp. 39–55. https://doi.org/10.1016/j.wocn.2018.06.001.

Nixon, Jessie S. and Fabian Tomaschek (2023). 'Does speech comprehension require phonemes?' The handbook of usage-based linguistics. John Wiley & Sons, Ltd. Chap. 9, pp. 161–178. https://doi.org/10.1002/9781119839859.ch9.

Norris, Dennis and James M. McQueen (2008). 'Shortlist B: A Bayesian model of continuous speech recognition'. Psychological review 115.2, pp. 357–395.

Oganian, Yulia, Ilina Bhaya-Grossman, Keith Johnson, and Edward F Chang (2023). 'Vowel and formant representation in the human auditory speech cortex'. Neuron 111.13, pp. 2105–2118.

Oh, Sejin, Jason A. Shaw, Karthik Durvasula, and Alexei Kochotov (2023). 'Russian assimilatory palatalization is incomplete neutralization'. Laboratory Phonology 15.1, pp. 1–37.

Öhman, Sven (2000). 'Expression and content in linguistic theory'. In The practice of language. Springer, pp. 99–107.

Payne, Elinor M. (2005). 'Phonetic variation in Italian consonant gemination'. Journal of the International Phonetic Association 35.2, pp. 153–181.

Peng, Shu-Hui (2000). 'Lexical versus "phonological" representations of Mandarin Sandhi tones'. Papers in laboratory phonology V: Acquisition and the lexicon. Ed. by Michael B. Broe and Janet B. Pierrehumbert. Cambridge: Cambridge University Press, pp. 152–167.

Piantadosi, Steven (2023). Modern language models refute Chomsky's approach to language. https://lingbuzz.net/lingbuzz/007180.

Pierrehumbert, Janet, Mary E. Beckman, and D. Robert Ladd (2000). 'Conceptual foundations of phonology as a laboratory science'. Phonological knowledge: Conceptual and empirical issues, pp. 273–304.

Pierrehumbert, Janet B. (2001). 'Why phonological constraints are so coarse-grained'. Language and cognitive processes 16.5–6, pp. 691–698.

Pierrehumbert, Janet B. (2002). 'Word-specific phonetics'. In Laboratory phonology 7. Ed. by Carlos Gussenhoven and Natasha Warner. Berlin: De Gruyter Mouton, pp. 101–140.

Pierrehumbert, Janet B. (2016). 'Phonological representation: Beyond abstract versus episodic'. Annual review of linguistics 2.1, pp. 33–52. https://doi.org.10.1146/annurev-linguistics-030514-125050.

Port, Robert F. (2007). 'The graphical basis of phones and phonemes'. In Language experience in second language speech learning: In honor of James Emil Flege. Ed by Ocke-Schwen Bohn and Murray Munro. Amsterdam: John Benjamins, 349–365.

Port, Robert F. and A. P. Leary (2005). 'Against formal phonology'. Journal of language 81.4, pp. 927–964. https://doi:10.1353/lan.2005.0195.

Port, Robert F. and Michael L. O'Dell (1985). 'Neutralization of syllable-final voicing in German'. Journal of phonetics 13.4, pp. 455–471. https://doi.org/10.1016/S0095-4470(19)30797-1.

Poser, William J. (1990). 'Evidence for foot structure in Japanese'. Language 66.1, pp. 78–105. https://doi.org.10.1353/lan.1990.0031.

Postal, Paul Martin (1968). 'Aspects of phonological theory'. New York: Harper & Row.

Prince, Alan and Paul Smolensky (1993/2004). Optimality theory: Constraint interaction in generative grammar. New York: Wiley-Blackwell.

Quine, Willard V. O. (1951). 'Two dogmas of empiricism'. Philosophical review 60.1, pp. 20–43. https://doi.org.10.2307/2266637.

R Core Team (2021). R. Version 1.4.1106. www.rstudio.com.

Reiss, Charles and Veno Volenec (2022). 'Conquer primal fear: Phonological features are innate and substance-free'. Canadian journal of linguistics/Revue canadienne de linguistique 67.4, pp. 581–610. https://doi.org.10.1017/cnj.2022.35.

Rialland, Annie. (1986). 'Schwa et syllabes en francais'. In Studies in compensatory lengthening. Ed. by Leo Wetzels and Engin Sezer. Dordrecht: Foris, pp. 186–226.

Roettger, T. B., B. Winter, S. Grawunder, J. Kirby, and M. Grice (2014). 'Assessing incomplete neutralization of final devoicing in German'. Journal of phonetics 43, pp. 11–25. https://doi.org/10.1016/j.wocn.2014.01.002.

Rundus, Dewey (1971). 'Analysis of rehearsal processes in free recall'. Journal of experimental psychology 89.1, p. 63.

Sagey, Elizabeth (1986). 'The representation of features and relations in non-linear phonology'. PhD diss. Cambridge, MA: MIT.

Schütze, Carson T. (1996). The empirical base of linguistics: Grammaticality judgments and linguistic I chicago: University of Chicago Press.

Silverman, Daniel (2006). A critical introduction to phonology: Of sound, mind, and body. London: Continuum.

Silverman, Daniel (2012). 'Mikołaj kruszewski: Theory and vision (part one)†'. Language and linguistics compass 6.6, pp. 330–342.

Sjerps, Matthias J., Neal P. Fox, Keith Johnson, and Edward F. Chang (2019). 'Speaker-normalized sound representations in the human auditory cortex'. Nature communications 10.1, p. 2465.

Skinner, B. F. (1957). 'Verbal behaviour'.

Slowiaczek, Louisa M. and Daniel A. Dinnsen (1985). 'On the neutralizing status of Polish word-final devoicing'. Journal of phonetics 13.3, pp. 325–341.

Slowiaczek, Louisa M. and Helena J. Szymanska (1989). 'Perception of word-final devoicing in Polish'. Journal of phonetics 17.3, pp. 205–212.

Steriade, Donca (1987). 'Redundant values'. CLS 23: Papers from the 23rd Annual Regional Meeting of the Chicago Linguistic Society. Part Two: Parasession on Autosegmental and Metrical Phonology. Ed. by Barbara Need, Anna Bosch, and Eric Schiller. Vol. 23.2. Chicago: Chicago Linguistic Society, pp. 339–362.

Tanner, James, Morgan Sonderegger, and Michael Wagner (2017). 'Production planning and coronal stop deletion in spontaneous speech'. Laboratory phonology: Journal of the association for laboratory phonology 8.1, p. 15. http://doi.org/10.5334/labphon.96.

Traunmüller, Hartmut (1990). 'Analytical expressions for the tonotopic sensory scale'. The journal of the acoustical society of America 88.1, pp. 97–100.

Trubetzkoy, Nikolai Sergeevich (1969). Principles of phonology. Berkeley: University of California Press.

Tucker, Benjamin V. and Natasha Warner (2010). 'What it means to be phonetic or phonological: The case of Romanian devoiced nasals'. Phonology 27.2, pp. 289–324.

Valian, Virginia (1982). 'Psycholinguistic experiment and linguistic intuition'. In Language, mind, and brain. Ed. by Thomas W. Simon and Robert J. Scholes. Hillsdale, NJ: Erlbaum, pp. 179–188.

Vallar, Giuseppe and Tim Shallice, eds (1990). 'Neuropsychological impairments of short-term memory'. In Chapters based on papers presented at a conference held in Villa Olmo, Como, Italy, Sep 14–16, 1987. Cambridge University Press.

Van Oostendorp, Marc (2008). 'Incomplete devoicing in formal phonology'. Lingua 118.9, pp. 1362–1374.

Vandenbussche, Erik, Rufin Vogels, and Guy A. Orban (1986). 'Human orientation discrimination: Changes with eccentricity in normal and amblyopic vision'. Investigative ophthalmology and visual science 27.2, pp. 237–245.

Volenec, Veno and Charles Reiss (2017). 'Cognitive phonetics: The transduction of distinctive features at the phonology-phonetics interface'. Biolinguistics 11. www.biolinguistics.eu/index.php/biolinguistics/article/view/509.

Wagner, M. (2012). 'Locality in phonology and production planning'. McGill working papers in linguistics 22.1, pp. 1–18. http://prosodylab.org/~chael/papers/wagner2012production.pdf.

Wagner, Michael (2002). 'The role of prosody in laryngeal neutralization'. MIT working papers in linguistics 42, pp. 373–392.

Wang, Yifeng and Jian Kang (1989). 'Hanyu fangyan de fenqu [The geographic division of Chinese dialects]'. Fangyan [Dialect] 4, p. 19.

Wang, Yifeng and Jian Kang (2012). 'Huai' an nanpian fangyan liangzizu lianxu biaodiao fenxi [An analysis of disyllabic tone sandhi in southern Huai' an dialect]'. Journal of Shenyang Institute of Engineering (Social Sciences) 8.3, pp. 357–359.

Wang, Yuedong (1998). 'Mixed effects smoothing spline analysis of variance'. Journal of the royal statistical society: Series b (statistical methodology) 60.1, pp. 159–174.

Warner, Natasha, Allard Jongman, Joan Sereno, and Rachèl Kemps (2004). 'Incomplete neutralization and other sub-phonemic durational differences in production and perception: Evidence from Dutch'. Journal of phonetics 32.2, pp. 251–276. https://doi.org/10.1016/S0095-4470(03)00032-9.

Waugh, Nancy C. and Donald A. Norman (1965). 'Primary memory'. Psychological review 72.2, p. 89.

Weber, Ernst Heinrich (1905). Tastsinn und gemeingefühl. Leipzig, Germany: Verlag von Wilhelm Englemann.

Wickham, Hadley, Mara Averick, Jennifer Bryan, Winston Chang, Lucy D'Agostino McGowan, Romain François, Garrett Grolemund, Alex Hayes, Lionel Henry, Jim Hester, et al. (2019). 'Welcome to the Tidyverse'. Journal of open source software 4.43, p. 1686.

Wiese, Richard (2000). The phonology of German. Oxford: Oxford University Press.

Wolpert, David H. and William G. Macready (1997). 'No free lunch theorems for optimization'. IEEE transactions on evolutionary computation 1.1, pp. 67–82.

Woo, Nancy Helen (1969). 'Prosody and phonology'. PhD diss. Cambridge, MA: Massachusetts Institute of Technology.

Wright, Richard (2004). 'Factors of lexical competition in vowel articulation'. In Phonetic interpretation: Papers in laboratory phonology VI. Ed. by J. Local, R. Ogden, and R. Temple. Cambridge: Cambridge University Press, pp. 75–87.

Xie, Xin, T. Florian Jaeger, and Chigusa Kurumada (2023). 'What we do (not) know about the mechanisms underlying adaptive speech perception: A computational framework and review'. Cortex 166, pp. 377–424. https://doi.org/10.1016/j.cortex.2023.05.003.

Xu, Yi (1993). 'Contextual tonal variation in Mandarin Chinese'. PhD diss. University of Connecticut.

Xu, Yi (1997). 'Contextual tonal variations in Mandarin'. Journal of phonetics 25.1, pp. 61–83.

Yang, Charles (2016). The price of productivity. Boston, MA: MIT press.

Yang, Jilin (2015). Zhongguo zhongxiaoxue baikequanshu [Encyclopedia for elementary school and middle school students]. Harbin Publishing House.

Yip, Moira (2002). Tone. Cambridge: Cambridge University Press.

Yu, Alan C. L. (2007). 'Understanding near mergers: The case of morphological tone in Cantonese'. Phonology 24.1, pp. 187–214.

Zellou, Georgia (2013). 'Consonant harmony in Moroccan Arabic: Similarity and incomplete neutralization'. The Journal of the Acoustical Society of America 133, pp. 3572. https://doi.org.10.1121/1.4806549.

Cambridge Elements

Phonology

Robert Kennedy
University of California, Santa Barbara

Robert Kennedy is a Senior Lecturer in Linguistics at the University of California, Santa Barbara. His research has focused on segmental and rhythmic alternations in reduplicative phonology, with an emphasis on interactions among stress patterns, morphological structure, and allomorphic phenomena, and sociophonological variation within and across the vowel systems of varieties of English. His work has appeared in *Linguistic Inquiry*, *Phonology*, and *American Speech*. He is also the author of *Phonology: A Coursebook* (Cambridge University Press), an introductory textbook for students of phonology.

Patrycja Strycharczuk
University of Manchester

Patrycja Strycharczuk is a Senior Lecturer in Linguistics and Quantitative Methods at the University of Manchester. Her research programme is centred on exploring the sound structure of language by using instrumental articulatory data. Her major research projects to date have examined the relationship between phonology and phonetics in the context of laryngeal processes, the morphology-phonetics interactions, and articulatory dynamics as a factor in sound change. The results of these investigations have appeared in journals such as the *Journal of Phonetics*, *Laboratory Phonology*, and *Journal of the Acoustical Society of America*. She has received funding from the British Academy and the Arts and Humanities Research Council.

Editorial Board
Diana Archangeli, *University of Arizona*
Ricardo Bermúdez-Otero, *University of Manchester*
Jennifer Cole, *Northwestern University*
Silke Hamann, *University of Amsterdam*

About the Series

Cambridge Elements in Phonology is an innovative series that presents the growth and trajectory of phonology and its advancements in theory and methods, through an exploration of a wide range of topics, including classical problems in phonology, typological and aerial phenomena, and interfaces and extensions of phonology to neighbouring disciplines.

Cambridge Elements⁼

Phonology

Elements in the Series

Coarticulation in Phonology
Georgia Zellou

Complexity in the Phonology of Tone
Lian-Hee Wee and Mingxing Li

Psycholinguistics and Phonology: The Forgotten Foundations of Generative Phonology
Naiyan Du and Karthik Durvasula

A full series listing is available at: www.cambridge.org/EPHO

For EU product safety concerns, contact us at Calle de José Abascal, 56–1°,
28003 Madrid, Spain or eugpsr@cambridge.org.

www.ingramcontent.com/pod-product-compliance
Lightning Source LLC
LaVergne TN
LVHW020349260326
834688LV00045B/1629